ELECTRONICS ABOARD

Stephen Fishman

Editor: Phyllis Klucinec

Bristol Fashion Publications, Inc.
Harrisburg, Pennsylvania

Electronics Aboard -- By Stephen Fishman

Published by Bristol Fashion Publications, Inc.

Copyright © 2001 by Stephen Fishman. All rights reserved.

No part of this book may be reproduced or used in any form or by any means-graphic, electronic, mechanical, including photocopying, recording, taping or information storage and retrieval systems-without written permission of the publisher.

BRISTOL FASHION PUBLICATIONS AND THE AUTHOR HAVE MADE EVERY EFFORT TO INSURE THE ACCURACY OF THE INFORMATION PROVIDED IN THIS BOOK BUT ASSUMES NO LIABILITY WHATSOEVER FOR SAID INFORMATION OR THE CONSEQUENCES OF USING THE INFORMATION PROVIDED IN THIS BOOK.

ISBN: 1-892216-40-X
LCCN: 2001-134041

Contribution acknowledgments

Inside Graphics: Stephen Fishman or As Noted
Cover Design: John P. Kaufman
Cover Graphic: Pinpoint Systems

Electronics Aboard -- By Stephen Fishman

Dedication

To my wife, Deborah, who understands my need to mess about with boats, and who knows she will always be my first love.

Acknowledgments

I wish to acknowledge Steve Bowden of Sea Tech Systems for his boundless enthusiasm and stream of conscious knowledge about all things electronic, if it can be useful aboard a boat. I will always fondly remember Mike and Kay DuBois of *Telltales Magazine,* who took a chance on me many years ago, and Jerry Renninger of *Southern Boating Magazine,* who introduced me to John Kaufman of Bristol Fashion Publications, Inc.

Electronics Aboard -- *By Stephen Fishman*

Electronics Aboard -- By Stephen Fishman

Preface
This Book's For You

So you've bought the boat of your dreams and she's everything you hoped she'd be, right? Well, maybe not EVERYthing. There are the Coast Guard minimums – PFDs, fire extinguishers, a bell and such. And, it would be awfully nice to have an anchor to keep from running into something while eating lunch or swimming. A stereo would be pretty cool, especially if it has a killer sound system like the one in your car. Then there are other creature comforts like a bimini or small refrigerator and, if you really want to do it right, air conditioning.

While you're out on the water, you'll want to appear completely in control and totally confident so your passengers can relax and enjoy the ride. Of course, it would also be great if you really DID know what you're doing.

I recommend that you take a boating safety and navigation course and gather the best help you can find. Surprisingly, some of the best crew is not human.

Your fourth cousin from way out west, who had to sit through eighth grade twice and thinks red tide is colored laundry detergent might be a great guy, but... The gorilla at work who thinks every problem can be solved with brute strength might one day get you out of a jam in high seas, but.... There is a plethora of electronics available to help ease your way and provide an elevated level of confidence even if you're new to boating.

Now, don't get me wrong. I like human companionship

Electronics Aboard -- By Stephen Fishman

as much as the next guy, maybe more than most. After all, it's far more satisfying to command a human being than to push buttons on a digital display, especially when the task is something you've done a zillion times.

On the other hand, if you actually LIKE doing stuff yourself and enjoy the independence that can come from boating with a small crew, or none at all, then you're the type of skipper who can benefit the most from the current crop of electronics for boats.

Today's marine electronics are more sophisticated and easier to use than ever. They provide more reliable navigation, longer-range communications and an increased level of safety for everyone on the water. There are also more manufacturers than ever before in the market place, offering more models and options in a constantly expanding range of prices.

No doubt about it, the price is down and the value is up when it comes to marine electronics – way up. But with so many models, how do you choose? What makes one depth sounder better than another? Why does one chart plotter costs $600 and another is four times as much? What's the deal with antennas? Can one manufacturer's autopilot connect to another vendor's GPS? The questions are as endless as the choices.

This book won't tell you which brand of radar you should buy, and it won't justify the expense of a higher priced radio over a cheaper one. What this book *will* do is help you become is a better-informed consumer and a more knowledgeable skipper the next time you consider adding to your on-board electronics. At a minimum, you'll be able to tell in a moment or two if a salesperson in a marine store knows what's what when it comes to marine electronics.

Okay. You've met the U.S Coast Guard safety minimums and you've even added a few extra PFDs. The bimini is in place over the cockpit so you won't fry your brains in the heat of the summer, the fridge is ready for your favorite drinks and now it's time to consider installing equipment that can make your boating life easier, safer and more enjoyable. So where do you start?

Electronics Aboard -- By Stephen Fishman

A VHF marine radio? A knot meter and depth sounder? After the basics, you might consider an autopilot. What autopilot would be complete without a GPS to tell it what to do? Why stop there? Why not a chart plotter or, at the very least, electronic charting software for your notebook computer? No portable computer? Well, what are you waiting for?

Going offshore? Don't leave home without a single sideband or a ham radio – or both! A satellite telephone would keep you in touch with your daughter at school while you're in the midst of a passage from St. Martin to Antigua. Whew!

Do you *need* all this stuff? Nope! Could you use all this stuff? Maybe. If you tried really hard. Would it make you a better skipper? Not a chance. But these gadgets *would* clutter up your cockpit and aggravate the devil out of you when they didn't work right. They will cost you a bundle and keep your local marine supplier VERY happy.

The most important thing, is that all this stuff would probably diminish the experience for you and everyone else on board. It would be pretty tough not to be preoccupied with buttons, dials, displays, interconnects and calibrations.

Unless you're going offshore alone, you just don't need it all, maybe not even then. You can sure use some of it even if you never leave the protection of the bay. Hopefully, what gear to buy and how to use it is what you'll get out of spending a few dollars for this book and a few hours reading it.

Stephen Fishman

Electronics Aboard -- *By Stephen Fishman*

Electronics Aboard -- By Stephen Fishman

Table of Contents

PREFACE   Page 7
    THIS BOOK'S FOR YOU

CHAPTER ONE   Page 15
    INTRODUCTION TO INSTRUMENTATION

CHAPTER TWO   Page 33
    SYSTEM INTEGRATION

CHAPTER THREE   Page 43
    DATA DISPLAYS

CHAPTER FOUR   Page 63
    VHF MARINE RADIOS

CHAPTER FIVE   Page 79
    FISHFINDERS

CHAPTER SIX   Page 91
    ELECTRONIC CHARTING

CHAPTER SEVEN   Page 101
    CHARTPLOTTERS

CHAPTER EIGHT   Page 117
    AUTOPILOTS

Electronics Aboard -- By Stephen Fishman

CHAPTER NINE   Page 131
    RADAR

CHAPTER TEN   Page 147
    LORAN C

CHAPTER ELEVEN   Page 163
    GPS

CHAPTER TWELVE   Page 181
    SINGLE SIDEBAND RADIOS

CHAPTER THIRTEEN   Page 201
    WEATHER FAX

CHAPTER FOURTEEN   Page 211
    THE WIRELESS OPTION

CHAPTER FIFTEEN   Page 223
    INSTALLATION ISSUES

CHAPTER SIXTEEN   Page 241
    NOTHING LASTS FOREVER

APPENDIX A   Page 243
    NAVIGATION & DISPLAY TERMINOLOGY

APPENDIX B   Page 255
    SATELLITE TELEPHONE GLOSSARY

APPENDIX C   Page 263
    TABLE OF FIGURES

Electronics Aboard -- *By Stephen Fishman*

Electronics Aboard -- By Stephen Fishman

Electronics Aboard -- By *Stephen Fishman*

Chapter One
Introduction To Instrumentation

Although I'm sure you know this already, I'd like to point out that powerboats and sailboats are different from each other. This might appear to be stating the obvious, but in truth, many of us lose sight of this when we talk about boating and being on the water. It's the differences in how our boats are used that determines what's needed to operate them safely and efficiently, and the underlying method that drives the sequence in which we equip our vessels.

For example, most motoryacht skippers spend only a small portion of a beautiful Saturday underway, preferring instead to travel from one local destination to another. By contrast, the typical sailboat and her crew are likely to keep moving most of the day, even if they have no particular place to go.

There are also different problems. While a sailboat skipper might be concerned about water depth or wind direction, the power yachtsman is likely to be more focused on the comfort of his passengers. This is not to say that sailors are bohemians, but it is true that most of the time spent on a sailboat is done so in an open cockpit at an angle of ten or twelve degrees. The powerboat crew spends their days in a vertical posture and, often, inside a temperature-controlled cabin while underway.

So, what's my point? Well, the point is, that although

Electronics Aboard -- By Stephen Fishman

powerboats and sailboats have much in common regarding equipment and instruments, there are distinct differences in vessel operation that drive the priorities of what instruments to buy, which are bought first, and where they are installed. If you look closely at the boats slipped on your dock, you'll likely find it difficult to miss the pattern that emerges – a sort of pecking order of instrument purchase and placement.

Not Exactly Feng Shui, But...

The ancient oriental art of object placement is considered by many to be a critical factor when arranging a room, or designing a house or office. It's said that the "Chi" – life's energy – will to flow more smoothly through our lives while helping us achieve our goals when our surroundings are arranged in a particular way. That may work at home, but on board it's tough to put a wall hanging in a specific spot, when the location just happens to be a cabin window or the door to the starboard deck.

Nonetheless, there's always a pattern to the way in which instruments are arranged, and with good reason. We must easily see the various gauges and displays. We need ready access to their controls. It's the instruments and their arrangement that can make or break our ability to safely and reliably operate our boats, regardless of weather and traffic.

The Basics

The "basics" include instruments that provide the minimum amount of information needed to safely operate the vessel. This will be different for each type of boat. For example, a jon boat fisherman might need nothing but a fishfinder and a fuel gauge, while a ski boat operator would be more likely to benefit from a knot meter and a fuel gauge. In both cases, the minimum requirement is a bit different but the results are the same. They have all the data they needed to operate their boats in a safe manner while they enjoy being on the water.

When it comes to larger vessels, things get a bit more complex. For the skipper of a thirty-foot sailboat, the basics might include a knot meter, a depth gauge and a wind direction indicator, but should absolutely include a marine VHF radio. For the same size powerboat, the minimum might be a knot meter, a fuel gauge and trim tab indicators, along with a marine VHF.

As vessels grow in size, the demands of safe operation call for a wider variety of instruments. As we venture further offshore, this minimum configuration also changes. As time at sea becomes longer even more instruments should be added to the mix. This doesn't include specialty instruments for activities such as deep sea fishing, treasure hunting, and so forth.

Without question, what you want to do, where you want to go and how long you will be away from home have a direct impact not only on which electronics you choose to buy, but also in which order they are purchased and how sophisticated they need to be. Further, both your actual and planned activities afloat will, to a great extent, determine where those instruments are installed.

Every skipper has a different vision of the perfect electronics array, but similarities can be drawn among vessels of a general size and type. This book is intended for the pleasure boater and, since the typical pleasure boat on navigable water in the United States is a 35-footer, let's take a look at what might be found aboard this typical vessel.

Don't worry about knowing anything about each device listed below. They are all discussed in detail in later chapters.

The Mid-Thirties Power Yacht

There are a wide variety of vessel styles within this general category, including express cruisers, cockpit motor-yachts, trawlers, performance boats, sportfishermen and open deck sport boats. Our typical 35-foot powerboat is a

Electronics Aboard -- By *Stephen Fishman*

motoryacht with a single steering station on the flybridge, dual engines and an open aft cockpit. This style of vessel is easy to operate, comfortable for crew and guests, and capable of going almost anywhere. It's also generally equipped with a full compliment of electronics.

There are two fundamental approaches to filling a helm with instruments:

- Review your needs and expectations, decide on which instruments to buy and then lay out their placement, even if they will be purchased over a period of time.
- Install instruments as you buy them, expecting to rearrange things, as needed, when additional electronics are added.

It shouldn't be too difficult to figure out which method is preferred. Planning for a fully-equipped helm helps prevent redundancy, manages the cost more effectively and allows you to install electronics in the best location – once.

The Antenna Farm

Since our typical yacht has an antenna arch spanning the flybridge, let's make good use of this by mounting all the antennas out of the way, and in the bargain, at the highest point on the ship. The antenna arch, also called a radar arch, will eventually support antennas for the VHF radio, the GPS receiver or the Loran-C, an open array radar and maybe even a wind speed indicator. If you plan to venture far offshore or for extended periods of time, consider allocating space for single sideband and satellite telephone antennas. If you must have your MTV, you have to plan for a television satellite dish.

Many antennas have specific needs regarding placement relative to other antennas, and this can be most easily accomplished if you know in advance what will eventually be installed.

Electronics Aboard -- By Stephen Fishman

Figure 1-1

Edson multiple antenna mount

If available space seems to be a problem, you can usually add an antenna mast, such as those offered by Edson Marine. Even so, antenna placement must still be considered since not all antennas work and play well with others.

At The Helm

On the flybridge, real estate is at even more of a premium than on the arch and the potential for electrical interference among instruments is fairly high. For these reasons, it's critical to plan where everything will go and which instruments will demand priority placement.

While it makes sense that the most important, or at least the most used, instruments should be given center stage, it doesn't always seem to work out that way. Often, electronics are installed in the order in which they're purchased, but planning ahead can help prevent difficulties in accessing controls and viewing multiple displays.

Aboard our typical 35-footer, the flybridge is not likely

to have a hard top but, instead, will usually have a canvas or vinyl bimini supported by a tubular stainless steel frame, firmly secured to the structure of the flybridge. Because a bimini is almost never removed, the overhead cross members of the frame are often used as mounting points for electronics with handsets or instruments with an LCD display.

Other mounting possibilities include the fiberglass or wood surface of the helm itself, as well as the interior of the helm by means of flush-mount adapters. Unless designed specifically for flush-mounting, most instruments are installed with a mounting bracket that permits easy surface-mounting where space is available. Although a surface-mount bracket is often used because it's much faster and easier to install, a flush-mount installation looks more elegant but demands precision layout and cutting.

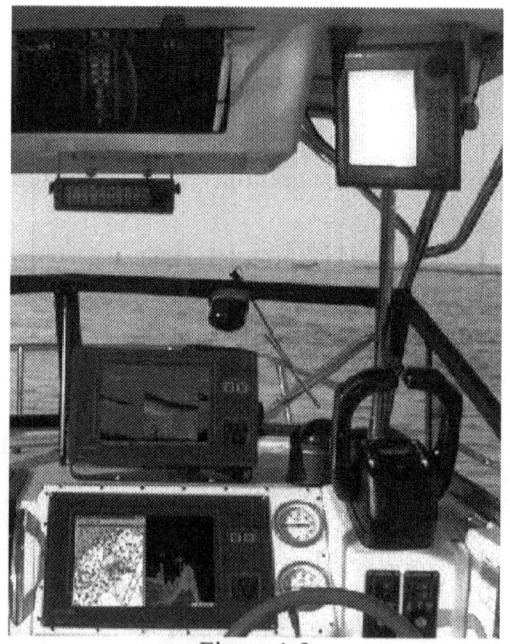

Figure 1-2

Surface-mount electronics

Electronics Aboard -- By Stephen Fishman

It's quite common to place a radar display and chartplotter directly in front of the steering wheel, while other devices such as speed, depth and fuel gauges are commonly flush-mounted into the helm. While important, these lesser electronics are not needed on a moment-to-moment basis since they monitor the vessel's status, but have little to do with navigating and ship's operations. As a result, they are relegated to a secondary location.

Figure 1-3

Modern flybridge instrumentation

Many newer vessels, particularly larger boats, are provided with an enclosure for most, if not all of the electronics you're likely to install. The flybridge of the 39-foot Bertram pictured above is a prime example of a well thought-out exterior helm, with ample space available for surface-mounted additions to the boatbuilder's electronics array.

Sample Configurations

Although they're not always used that way, most people buy boats with the expectation of making long weekend

Electronics Aboard -- By Stephen Fishman

trips and an occasional extended cruise. The electronics are always a part of this preparation. How long and far the cruise will take the crew are factors that drive decisions about how extensive the instrumentation should be. Presented below are two configurations that address this issue, the first being for a long weekend cruise, and the other for the offshore voyager.

A Long Weekend

Navigation electronics for a long weekend away from the dock, and possibly some time spent out of sight of land, requires you to be prepared, but generally lacks the need for extensive communications devices. Given that, here is a recommended setup for a three to four day trip, bearing in mind that the motoryacht we're fitting out is a 35-footer that is likely to be operated only in generally fair weather.

- A fixed-mount and a handheld marine VHF radios
- Knot and depth gauges
- Autopilot, preferably a hydraulic below-deck type
- Radar with an open array antenna
- GPS with differential correction, or a Loran-C receiver
- Perhaps a cellular telephone

Figure 1-4

Electronics for a short cruise

An Extended Cruise

The primary difference between preparing for a long weekend at sea and an open-ended cruise is the issue of

Electronics Aboard -- By Stephen Fishman

communications. Staying in touch with family and friends is certainly important, but even more critical is being able to communicate with other cruisers and, should the need arise, rescue authorities.

If you were to take a poll of concerns people have about going to sea, the largest category would be comprised of issues that threaten the safety of the vessel and, by extension, human life. Skippers often focus on creature comforts such as air conditioning and the power needed to keep it running, satellite television and so forth, but they worry most about coming back alive and well. To that end, boat owners, bent on a long cruise, will also invest in a liferaft, a ditch bag, a high-end dinghy and, without exception, extensive communications electronics.

A prudent skipper will never go to sea without a full compliment of lifesaving instruments that can help prevent a disaster or aid another vessel found in dire straits. The compliment of instrumentation for a 35-footer venturing offshore may look like this:

- A fixed-mount and a handheld marine VHF radios
- Knot and depth gauges with large displays at the helm
- Autopilot, a hydraulic below-deck type with both a remote and a fixed-mount control
- Radar with an open array antenna
- DGPS with WAAS integration
- Chartplotter
- Single sideband radio
- Weather fax
- Satellite telephone
- Repeaters, in the cabin, for the primary navigation instruments

Electronics Aboard -- By Stephen Fishman

AT THE HELM

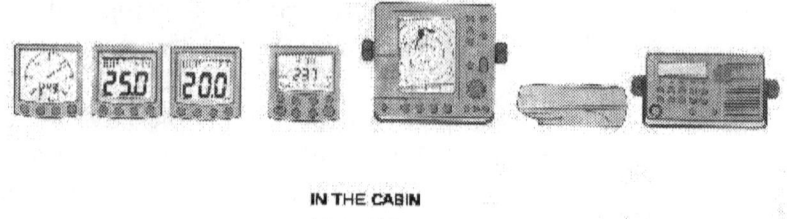

IN THE CABIN

Figure 1-5

Electronics for an extended cruise

The primary difference between the two configurations is communications, and therein also lies much of the differences in cost. The suggested electronics configuration for a long weekend away will help keep a crew *out* of trouble, while the configuration for an extended cruise is meant to help the crew *deal* with trouble. The difference in cost is significant, but if you're going to be on your own for weeks at a time, there is no substitute for being prepared.

The Mid-Thirties Sailboat

Unlike powerboats, cruising sailboats have more standardized designs and, although there are certainly differences in styling, vessel styles can generally be divided into two categories – aft cockpit and center cockpit yachts. Discounting the newer cruising catamarans, our typical 35-foot sailboat has an aft cockpit with wheel steering as opposed to a tiller, a diesel engine and is sloop-rigged. Like its powerboat cousins, a 35-foot sailboat is easy to operate, comfortable for crew and guests, and capable of going most anywhere in the world.

Electronics Aboard -- By Stephen Fishman

Like its counterpart in the motoryacht world, a sailboat is also generally equipped with a full compliment of electronics, requiring the same considerations of forethought and planning.

Antennas

Although an antenna arch is a common feature of larger sailing vessels, a mid-thirties sailboat is rarely configured with an antenna arch. Instead, antennas are installed in several places around the boat, each taking advantage of whatever that particular location has to offer.

A sailboat of this size has a masthead about 50 feet off the water, so the top of the mast is the best place for the VHF radio antenna and a wind machine transducer. The front of the mast, somewhere above the first spreader, is a common location for a radome, along with a radar reflector. A single sideband antenna, if present, is usually attached to the backstay and a Loran-C antenna might be mounted to the stern rail of the cockpit. Plans that take you far offshore might be more pleasurable with a satellite TV dish fastened to the top of a short mast on the transom.

As mentioned before, each antenna has specific needs regarding placement relative to other antennas, and a mid-thirties sailboat offers ready accommodations to satisfy these needs.

In The Cockpit

The real estate available for electronics in the cockpit of a sailboat is usually more limited than aboard a powerboat. This increases the potential for electrical interference among instruments. Therefore, it's absolutely essential to plan what you will buy and how those devices will be installed.

The instrument arrangement aboard a sailboat should be designed to provide maximum visibility, even at odd angles to the display, since a sailboat is rarely steered from directly

Electronics Aboard -- *By Stephen Fishman*

behind the wheel. Instead, the helmsman usually stands or sits thirty to forty degrees off the centerline. This requires one of three conditions must exist - either the instruments must be located forward in the cockpit, there must be redundant displays forward of the helm, or the displays themselves must provide a wide viewing angle. The technology of today's electronics makes the third option not only possible, but preferable, even given the somewhat higher costs. Nonetheless, this would still be my first choice since it simplifies other considerations.

Like the motoryacht, a cruising sailboat usually has a canvas bimini supported by a tubular stainless steel frame. Unlike a powerboat, the bimini on a sailboat is rarely used as an attachment point for mounting electronics. A sailing bimini has a lower clearance than a bimini on a motoryacht and the bimini must be removed, or at least lowered, for periodic sail removal and rigging maintenance.

Pedestal guards are the preferred location for electronics, and they are generally available in two styles – a straight guard and a double-bend guard. A straight pedestal guard lends itself to a single large display along with one or two smaller instruments on accessory arms, while a guard with a compound bend can handle two large displays. This is most easily accomplished through the use of instrument pods, or housings, that accept most currently available instruments made with LCD displays, including large electronics such as radar displays, chartplotters and fishfinders.

It's common practice to install a radar display or chartplotter in the upper portion of a compound guard, with knot, depth and wind gauges mounted beneath. If an autopilot control is also installed here, the knot and depth gauges can be combined into a single unit with two displays. If an installation calls for both a radar display and a chartplotter to be attached to the guard, other gauges can be mounted on accessory arms.

Electronics Aboard -- By Stephen Fishman

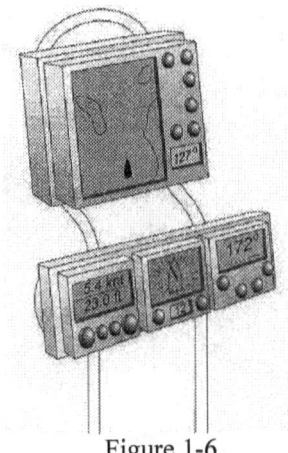

Figure 1-6

Instruments mounted on a pedestal guard

Figure 1-7

Enclosed sailboat helm

    Similar to the helm on powerboats, many newer, larger sailing vessels are equipped with an enclosed pedestal guard and helm that allows flush-mounting of all instruments. Figure 7 is a good example of an enclosed helm used to the best advantage.

Electronics Aboard -- By Stephen Fishman

On Deck

On many traditional sailboats, the cockpit is rather small and doesn't lend itself to substantial electronics installations. For these vessels, instrument housings mounted across the companionway are often the best choice. Sailing craft with canoe-sterns, such as Hans Christian and Tayana, are good examples of sailboats that can benefit from locating the instrument cluster forward of the cockpit.

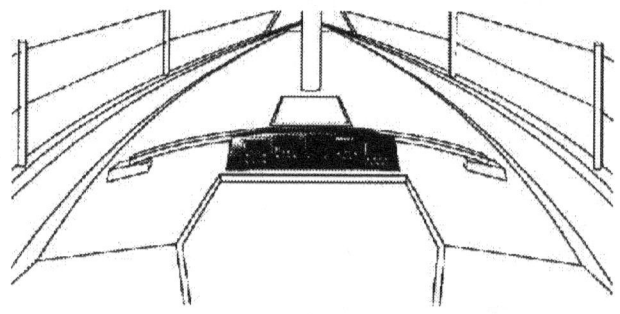

Figure 1-8

Instrument installations forward of the cockpit

Some racing skippers insist on installing electronics both in the cockpit and across the companionway in an effort to make sure all crew can see them. It's quite common to see instruments mounted aboard racing sailboats on the mast beneath the boom, stacked vertically, to provide high visibility of the instruments for the entire crew.

Sailboat Configurations

Like motoryachts, most people who buy sailboats do so with the intent of making occasional long weekend trips and an extended cruise or two. How far offshore you plan to go and for how long is the driving force behind any electronics purchase. Unlike a motoryacht, however, the electronics of a

Electronics Aboard -- By Stephen Fishman

sailboat are usually split between the cockpit and the cabin.

On deck, the helmsman on a sailboat is likely to see little other than navigation instruments, while most of the communications gear is installed belowdecks. There should always be at least a marine VHF radio close at hand in the cockpit, but more sophisticated devices such as a single sideband, a weather fax or a ham radio will, invariably, remain in the cabin. For this reason, many sailboat owners find it prudent to install repeaters in the cabin.

Repeaters are displays that offer the same information that the helmsman sees, but without the controls. Repeaters keep off-watch crew informed of the ship's operations, and can relay course and speed data to a second or third crew member during extended communications sessions with other boaters and maritime authorities.

Below are two configurations of electronics for sailboats that address the long weekend cruise and an offshore voyage.

A Long Weekend Away

As mentioned before, a long weekend away requires that you be prepared but typically doesn't include elaborate communications devices. Listed below is an array of electronics for a 35-foot sailboat heading out for a long weekend in predictably good weather.

- A fixed-mount and a handheld marine VHF radios
- Knot and depth gauges
- Wind machine, displaying direction and wind speed
- Autopilot, probably a wheel pilot
- A differential GPS or Loran-C receiver
- Perhaps a cell phone

For a long weekend away, the electronics plan is not much more than you might already have aboard for a daysail or an overnight in protected waters.

Electronics Aboard -- By Stephen Fishman

An Extended Voyage

Communications devices are the primary difference between preparing for a long weekend and an open-ended cruise, but now it becomes important to also consider two other issues. The chance of encountering bad weather and the need for more sophisticated navigation assistance. You must be able to communicate with other cruisers, as well as high seas authorities, and electronic charting can make the cruise more enjoyable and safer.

Like any skipper venturing out on the open ocean, you need to be concerned about the safety of your vessel and its crew. I would much rather go to sea with creature comforts than without them, but a liferaft, ditch bag and a good dinghy should also be aboard.

As I've said before, a prudent skipper will never go to sea without a full compliment of communications and navigation aids. These considerations drive my suggested list of instrumentation for heading offshore aboard a 35-foot sailboat.

- Two marine VHF radios, a fixed-mount and a hand-held at the helm, and a second fixed-mount belowdecks
- Knot and depth gauges with large displays at the helm, and a combined second display below
- Autopilot, either wheel pilot or a hydraulic below-deck type, but with one control at the helm and another in the cabin
- Radar with a radome antenna installed on a mast-mounted gimbal
- DGPS with WAAS
- Chartplotter
- Single sideband radio
- Weather fax
- Satellite telephone
- Repeaters at the chart table of primary navigation instruments

Electronics Aboard -- By Stephen Fishman

The primary differences here are communications and redundancy. Once again, the difference in cost is significant but, in my opinion, only a fool would go to sea unprepared.
For me, preparation is a combination of significant experience and proper equipment, and there is no substitute for either.

Installation Reminders

Whether power or sail, any installation that includes several instruments demands proper grounding to avoid electrical interference among devices, as well as to prevent electrical shock. Proper grounding includes the use of a common bus for the attachment of the black (ground, negative) wire of a two-wire 12-volt DC pair. It may also include an extensive copper groundplane for communications devices such as a single sideband radio.

If you're planning to use surface-mount brackets to install some or all of your electronics, be certain to seal the opening where the wiring from the device passes through the material to which it is attached. The hole can be filled with silicone caulk, or you can use a fitting like the one shown, but it must be done in a way that prevents any chance of water entry around the wiring.

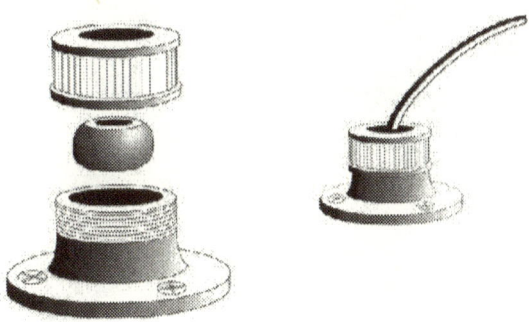

Figure 1-9

Surface-mount wiring seal

Electronics Aboard -- *By Stephen Fishman*

A surface fitting is a two-part piece of hardware housing a rubber grommet that compresses against the wires as the top is tightened against the base. The grommet not only prevents moisture entry, it also limits the movement of the wiring so it can't be easily pulled out. The base, fastened to the surface with small screws and bedded with silicone or caulk, can be installed either horizontally or vertically and is equally effective in both modes. You may consider this to be an extra (and unnecessary) expense, but it is less likely to leak and is more attractive than an exposed hole.

Chapter Two
System Integration

In recent years, one of the most convenient methods of connecting many instruments together has been the evolution of complete navigation packages from a single vendor. While this approach is undoubtedly profitable for the manufacturer, it can also benefit the average skipper by reducing the number of variables in interconnectivity and compatibility of instruments. Examples of this approach can be seen in products from Raymarine, Furuno and Simrad, among others.

One of the better-known examples of this single-source approach is provided by Raytheon (now Raymarine) in their *Autohelm* brand products. All of their instruments – autopilot, GPS, radar, chartplotters, sailing instruments, powerboat displays - talk to each other using a single style connector and a common language protocol called *SeaTalk®*. When a single vendor's products are used, the configuration time and effort is less than if different manufacturer's products are intermixed. This means you can install the equipment and begin using it more quickly.

A single-source supplier isn't necessarily better than assembling products from many sources but it can be less frustrating. At the very least, there is only one company to deal with if problems occur.

There are three basic approaches to navigation instrument integration – NMEA, proprietary systems, and local area networks. Each approach offers benefits to the skipper - cost savings, ease of installation and setup, or flexibility in future expansions – and can often overlap or be used in conjunction with each other.

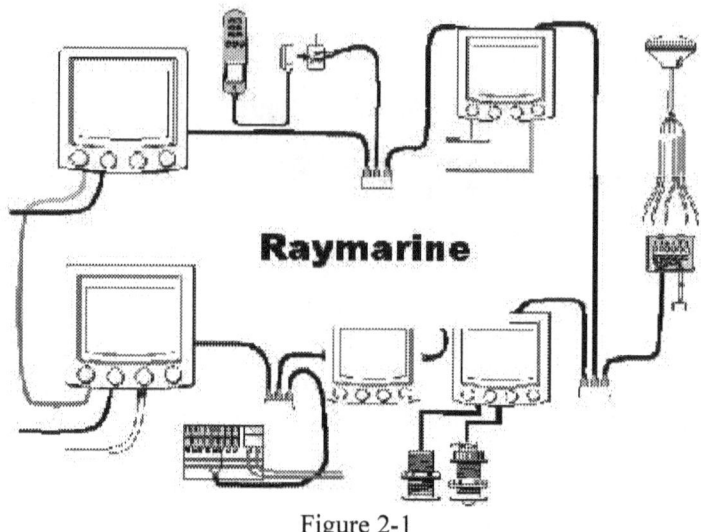

Figure 2-1

Raymarine's Autohelm system

NMEA Communications

One approach is to use instruments equipped with an NMEA0183 (National Marine Electronics Association) interface. This is an industry-standard communication protocol for marine electronics products which allows instruments from different manufacturers to talk to each other. For example, NMEA provides a way for your new Furuno GPS to send instructions to the Autohelm autopilot you already have on board. This protocol is especially useful if you regularly download waypoint information to a GPS from a notebook computer.

Electronics Aboard -- By Stephen Fishman

Cabling

Data is sent from one instrument to another along a three-wire cable that can be configured with a wide array of connectors. For a notebook computer, the connection is made to the serial port by means of a DB9 (9-pin RS232) fitting.

Instruments can also be made to communicate with each other without connectors. This technique is called hard wiring but presents potential difficulties if the need arises to change the configuration or remove a device for service.

In this scenario, an instrument, such as an autopilot, would be connected to an NMEA bus by the same three wires used for a DB9 connector. However, instead of a connector, the wiring goes directly to the device and is held in place with solder, mechanical connectors or screws.

Bending a wire around the shaft of a screw and tightening the fastener offers much easier installation and removal, but presents the greatest opportunity for a poor contact to develop as a result of moisture, corrosion or vibration.

Proprietary Systems

SeaTalk

A second approach is to use instruments from only one manufacturer. Raymarine's SeaTalk system offers a common cabling scheme and communication method. This allows you to interconnect all instruments within a single model family, such as their Autohelm ST40 series that includes a an autopilot, GPS, sailing instruments and more.

However, it restricts your choices of instruments to only those products with the appropriate proprietary interface and built-in software. Luckily, the vendors who offer this type of solution also offer a host of options and models in the hope you won't look elsewhere for upgrades and replacements.

Electronics Aboard -- By *Stephen Fishman*

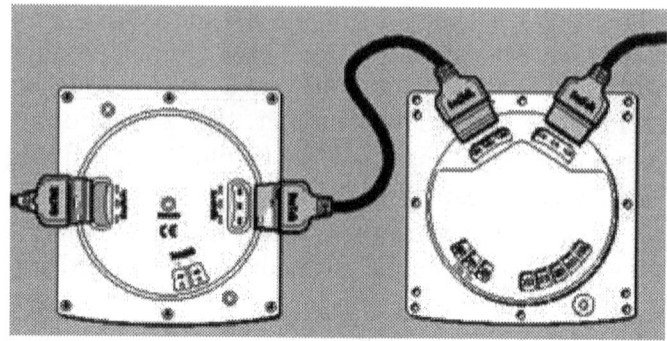

Figure 2-2

SeaTalk wiring

Cabling

Like their protocols, these proprietary systems use a cabling configuration that is unique to their "network" of devices. In the case of Raymarine, all of their ST series instruments are connected to each other by means of a connecting system that is color-coded and built into the rear of each instrument. Although these same instruments would also work well in an NMEA environment, the simplest installation results from using only their products and taking advantage of the SeaTalk protocol.

Local Area Networks

Another way to deal with networking is to set up a network. Furuno offers a system called NavNet that uses standard components from the world of PC local area network products. NavNet assembles Ethernet 10-base T cables, routers and hubs to form networks that are the fastest onboard systems currently available.

Electronics Aboard -- By Stephen Fishman

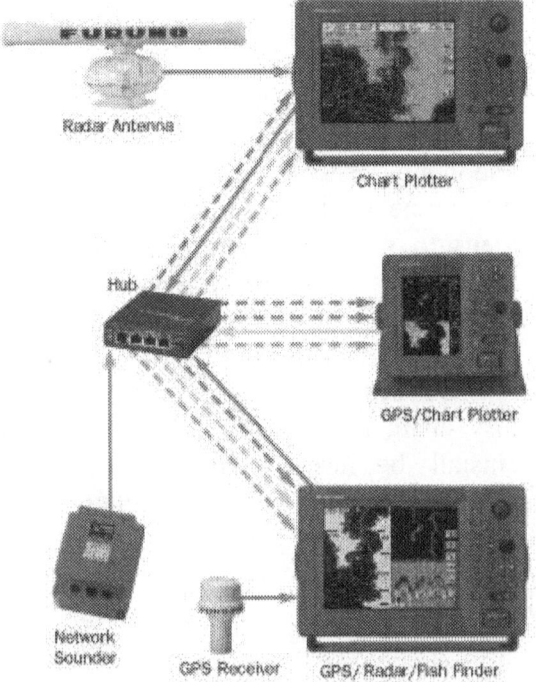

Figure 2-3

Furuno NavNet

Ethernet is a mature methodology of network hardware technology and software protocols. It can operate at data speeds of 10 megabytes per second (10MBPS) and up to 1 gigabyte per second (1GBPS). What this means to you is essentially three things – it's the fastest marine network out there, by design it has almost limitless expansion potential, and it's likely to be well supported for a long time to come.

One of the greatest strengths of a true LAN is the plethora of sources from which components can be bought. Although only Furuno supplies the NavNet operating system, the hardware components necessary to assemble an Ethernet network are available from hundreds of computer retailers and mail order suppliers.

Electronics Aboard -- By Stephen Fishman

Cabling

Most Ethernet networks use the same RG-59 coaxial cable as television cable. The ends of the cables terminate with either a BNC connector or an RJ-46 (which looks like an overgrown telephone connector).

A BNC connector has a female bayonet fitting on each end that fastens to a male counterpart on a "T-connector" which, in turn, is located on a computer or instrument. A T-connector has two male fittings, providing a way of attaching two cables. Ethernet lends itself to two cable topologies – a "daisy chain" and a "wheel."

A daisy chain (also called an end-to-end system), is simple to install because it doesn't matter where the instruments are located relative to each other. You simply use cables of the appropriate lengths to make the runs from one device to another until all the devices are connected. A daisy chain network invariably includes T-connectors and BNC end fittings.

Figure 2-4

Ethernet BNC connector

If RJ-46 phone connectors are used, there is only one connecting point on the computer or device, so a central connecting point is needed. An RJ-46 network uses a "wheel" topology, employing a hub - a small box with multiple cable connections - to which all cables are connected. Instead of running cables from one instrument to the next, cables are run from each device to one of several ports on the hub. More often than not, a phone jack connector is used when installing a wheel topology. It is this cable configuration that Furuno's NavNet uses. If you or your technician know what you're doing, a true network may be your best approach.

One Caution

Whether you use RG-59 BNC connectors or RJ-46 phone connectors, moisture entry at the connection is a common problem. Both connections leave much to be desired when it comes to preventing salty, moist air from corroding the contacts on the network connectors. As a result, it's critical that you take precautions. As always, if they are going to fail, network connections are almost certain to fail at the most inopportune time.

The most common method of preventing connector corrosion is to surround the entire connector and socket with clear silicone. After inserting the end of the cable into its receptacle, force silicone into gaps and crevices by applying far more material than you would ever consider using. When the silicone has cured, it will provide an airtight, moisture-free connection that can absorb the shock of wind and waves.

Note: *Replace these silicone blobs at least annually, but inspect the connections quarterly, especially if you spend a lot of time on open water.*

Whether it's NavNet or another Ethernet network, a proprietary system or something you've cobbled together, virtually all instruments can be connected for data exchange in one way or another. As a result, you can expect to accomplish several goals:

- Display images from different devices on one or two shared monitors
- Operate all connected instruments from one or two common keypads or controllers
- Create split-screen displays
- Overlay the images of two or more devices onto a single LCD or CRT display
- Use both Navionics® and C-Map® electronic charts
- Display images from video cameras in various locations aboard the vessel, such as in the engine compartment or at the location of a critical through-hull valve

Other Systems

High Speed Bus (HSB)

While NavNet is driven by proprietary software, Raymarine's HSB is based on a proprietary single-wire network cabling topology. Unlike NavNet which is usable with just about any instrument that can be connected with an Ethernet cable, HSB is confined to only a small portion of Raytheon's product line. This includes only the Pathfinder series of displays, radar and chartplotters.

HSB provides a way for two radar units to communicate with each other, or to connect two displays to a single radar and have the displays share information with each other. In this system, one HSB display can show a radar image and a chartplotter image on one screen as an overlay of the two images. This is significantly different from most other systems that use a single display to show a radar image and chartplotter image side-by-side as a split-screen display.

RS-232 Serial

An RS-232 serial connection has been in use for more than 30 years, and has been applied in three fundamental areas of computer science:

- As a means of communicating between computers sharing a common operating system
- As a method of communicating among dissimilar computers using mutually incompatible operating systems
- As a convenient way of using and sharing computer-related accessories

In decades past, there were two serial connector configurations built into computers and accessories - a 25-pin male connector (DB-25) and a 9-pin male connector (DB-9). The 25-pin serial connector was designed as a male connector in order to avoid confusion with a parallel printer cable connector, which is a 25-pin female, also called a DB-25. Even today, a parallel cable connector on virtually any computer – PC or Macintosh, desktop or portable - is still a DB-25 female connector.

Figure 2-5

DB-25 male connector

The DB-25 configuration has all but disappeared for networking. The DB-9 connector continues to be a viable serial terminator for many types of products for two reasons. The cabling requires as few as three wires, and the protocol is well-known and easily configured. A good example of this is what a telephone modem looked like.

Until the early 1980s, a modem was literally a telephone handset placed in a cradle that was connected to the computer. All communication took place using the built-in

Electronics Aboard -- By Stephen Fishman

microphone and ear receiver of the telephone's handset. As recently as 10 years ago, many computer users were still using external modems that connected to the rear of the computer. These small, thin boxes produced the same funny noises that internal modems continue to make in our modern computers.

Funny noises notwithstanding, these external modems provided a way to configure incoming information in a way that allowed the serial port to pass the data to its host computer. In return, the modem could also send information out to a modem on the other end of the connection. These protocols were sometimes configured on the fly by intelligent modems but, more commonly, were set up ahead of time by the computer operator. In addition to being a standardized system of cabling and connectors, RS-232 serial is a protocol that simplifies the task of getting devices from different manufacturers to talk to each other.

Times have certainly changed, but the RS-232 serial protocol continues to be a viable way of communicating among disparate devices, and this is the basis of several emerging marine network schemes.

Electronics Aboard -- By Stephen Fishman

Chapter Three
Data Displays

FSTN. LCD. CRT. Active matrix. VGA. LED. Pixel. TFT. Interlaced. Do any of these terms mean anything to you? If they don't, you're not alone.

During the last two decades, computer technology has matured at an incredible rate, giving us faster processors (up to 1.5 Ghz as of this writing), greater memory capacity (many gigabytes of RAM), program storage cartridges (EPROMS) and simple controls, while the size of these units shrink in size and cost. But of all the advances in computer technology, the component that has been the slowest to change has been the display.

As far back as the early 1980s, marine communication and navigation equipment began borrowing technology from the fledgling personal computer market and it continues today. In fact, the greatest advances in navigation electronics owe virtually all of their functionality to the micro-miniaturization that made PCs possible. This can easily be seen in the products on dealers' shelves or in the catalogues of marine suppliers. Physically small, feature-rich, relatively easy to use devices that provide instant answers to difficult questions.

While computers were getting faster – even in the late 1970s – displays were still showing us monochrome green screens on a device called a cathode ray tube, or CRT. This was, and still is, a high-resolution image using essentially the same technology as the black and white televisions many of us grew up with.

Electronics Aboard -- By *Stephen Fishman*

Figure 3-1

Monochrome green CRT display

Then came amber monochrome CRTs, in the mid-1980s. These were easier on your eyes but still a far cry from what the average user wanted, which was a color image like TV. The problem was, the TV at home was a low-resolution display that couldn't begin to match the sharpness of detail and crispness provided by a computer-generated CRT image.

Meanwhile in the mid-1970s, LEDs – light emitting diodes – began showing up in devices such as calculators, wrist watches and clocks. These were bright and easy to read and required little, power but were limited to relatively simple information displays. Nonetheless, LEDs were the first flat-screen displays that, in miniature, paved the way for future improvements.

One of the drawbacks to LEDs has always been the fact that the digits must be manufactured in a specific size, typically to satisfy a specific purpose. If the display is one-inch tall it will always be one-inch tall and can't be reconfigured to a different display size.

Electronics Aboard -- By Stephen Fishman

Figure 3-2

LED multiple display

In addition to the fact that a larger power source is needed to operate an LED device as compared with other display options, the issue of an unchangeable display size motivated electronics engineers to find a better way. Even so, there are still many products we use everyday that incorporate an LED display, but almost all of them run on 110 volt AC household current instead of batteries. No doubt many examples come to mind, including microwave and convection ovens, coffee makers, audio components, televisions, clocks and so forth.

Enter Color

The first truly good color computer monitors were introduced by Princeton Graphics in 1981. This laid the foundation of ongoing changes in display technology that still continues. These were not high-resolution displays - even though they were called enhanced graphics adapters (EGA) - but they were bright 14-inch color CRT screens offering a one-pixel display that simulated something approaching high-resolution. These monitors looked a lot like oddly-shaped portable televisions but they were fairly expensive, being several times more costly than portable televisions of the time.

Fast-forward a few years and the first liquid crystal displays (LCDs) began to appear on laptop computers from such makers as Toshiba and NEC. These amber monochrome LCDs offered several distinct advantages over their CRT

Electronics Aboard -- By Stephen Fishman

brethren. They were far less expensive to build, they could be made very thin and they required far less energy for their operation. All of a sudden, reasonably priced portable computers could be a reality.

LCDs borrowed some ideas from their elder LED relatives, but the technology that made LCD displays possible was brand new. It was based, to a large degree, on a design idea that had been around for millions of years – the human eye.

A Lesson From Nature

The retina is a light-sensitive membrane in the back of the eye containing "rods" and "cones" that receive an image from the lens and send it to the brain through the optic nerve. A few decades ago, electronics designers began looking at the retina and decided to use it as a model for computer displays. Rods in the retina are not color-sensitive but see only in black and white, responding to light and dark intensity only. They are scattered over the entire surface of the retina but predominate in the outer areas, providing peripheral vision. We think we see color in our peripheral vision because our brains interpolate – fill in the blanks, so to speak – and extend to the outer edges of our vision what we really *do* see in color in the central area.

Cones, on the other hand, are our color sensors but they are very specialized in that they see only one of three colors – red, green or blue. There are zillions of closely-spaced cones on the surface of the retina that act as a single mass of light-sensitive color receptors, with the result that we see in zillions of shades of colors.

The idea of hundreds of thousands of closely-spaced individual receptors formed the basis for LCD displays. These display receptors, called pixels, receive power individually but act in concert to provide the impression of smooth transitions of tone and color. For years, this concept has formed the basis of color CRT technology in commercial, military and consumer products such as television and visual scanning devices.

Electronics Aboard -- By Stephen Fishman

Modern science wasn't the first group to understand this physiology and put it to use. The impressionist painters of Europe applied this idea to their work and, for many years, created arresting scenes comprised of thousands of dots of paint which appeared to be a unified whole when viewed from a few feet away.

A subset of impressionism was a small group that called themselves Pointillists. Pointillism took this technique of color dots one step further by developing ways to control the diameter, the size of each dot of paint. The results were stunning, incredibly realistic images that give the impression of being accomplished by a camera instead of a brush.

It wasn't long before these new LCD displays were also made in color, but there were two problems. The first was that portable computers that sported a color LCD cost a king's ransom by comparison with their monochrome display cousins. This, once again, put most of these wonderful new machines out of the price range of the typical business user, let alone the average consumer.

The other problem was, the color LCDs had a very limited range of color capability. An LCD monitor for a personal computer can display at least 256 colors but a color LCD display on a high-end marine navigation device will still only show 16 colors. Unless you're willing to empty your wallet, you won't be able to afford the color LCDs that offer a full color range. At least not yet.

In the meantime, CRT display technology has been doing anything but standing still. The screens have gotten larger, the resolution continues to increase and the potential number of colors than can be displayed has grown to 16 million shades or more. Most color monitors these days are non-interlaced displays that allow for large screens while still maintaining a high-resolution image.

Electronics Aboard -- By *Stephen Fishman*

Figure 3-3

Modern LCD color display

Within the last decade came something to get excited about - a TFT color display. This new thin film transistor (TFT) technology combined the best that electronic displays had to offer. It was a high-resolution (800x600) flat-screen LCD that could be made very thin (1/2"). It was bright and required far less power than a conventional LCD display. Best of all, it could be sold at a price that made it attractive to consumers. What a deal!

At the time of this writing, active matrix TFT displays are beginning to close the high-resolution gap with CRTs which can achieve resolutions of up to 1240x780, and more. No doubt this trend will continue with TFT - or some other yet-to-be-invented flat screen color technology – eventually giving us wall-mounted, very high definition televisions that may displace the notion of a dedicated computer display.

But I Digress...

In the good old days, when the black and white television in our house went on the fritz, which was fairly

Electronics Aboard -- By Stephen Fishman

often, it was my job to remove the fiberboard rear cover and put on my TV repairman hat. Like most families, we had a tube tester and, one by one, each tube on the chassis was removed and plugged into the appropriate socket on the test panel. When I found which tube had gone bad, I went to the local hardware store for a replacement. Within minutes of returning home, the television was once again alive and well.

These were still the days of vacuum tubes, and even most radios weren't transistorized. The interesting thing is, some things haven't changed. If you think vacuum tubes have gone the way of the dodo bird, think again. One of the most popular modern appliances uses a vacuum tube and will likely continue to do so for the foreseeable future. To be precise, there are four instances of vacuum tubes that no manner of technology has been able to displace – yet.

Can you name them? How *about* television? The picture that we're looking at for far too long every day is a vacuum tube. Until high-definition TFT color technology (or something similar) is developed and marketed at a price we can all afford, our televisions will almost certainly continue to be a vacuum tube.

How about the microwave oven we all like so much? What makes it possible is a microwave vacuum tube that emits invisible energy.

If you work in an office, you come in contact with perhaps the most common vacuum tube of all, fluorescent lighting. Whether you work at home or simply live there, you no doubt have incandescent lighting – light bulbs – in several fixtures throughout the house. These are all vacuum tubes that, eventually, will be usurped by other illumination devices. In the meantime, for all of our technology advances we are still using some very old technology. We're just using it a lot better than we used to.

Interestingly, in some respects, we seem to have come full circle. One of the most advanced types of displays currently available is the FSTN display. Significantly, it's a monochrome display but, perhaps most importantly, is the fact

Electronics Aboard -- By Stephen Fishman

that it's a high-resolution LCD flat-screen display that can be easily seen in bright sunlight. The viewing angle provided by these displays is so broad that you don't have to be directly in front of a screen to see it clearly.

These FSTN (film super twisted nematic) displays are showing up in gadgets ranging from handheld communications devices to portable video games.

So, what's all this mean to the average skipper? Plenty. Among other things, it means there's some incredible technology available that can, and is, being applied to the world of electronic navigation.

For example, even Raytheon's lowest price radar sports an FSTN monochrome display capable of four grayscales and a moderate resolution of 320 x 240 pixels on a 7 inch screen. Given the price, that's a lot of radar for the money. On the other end of the product scale, they offer a high-end radar that delivers a full VGA display in a flat-screen LCD of 16 colors produced by more than 300,000 pixels. This screen can be seen in full sunlight from almost anywhere in the cockpit. And Raytheon is not alone.

Most major manufacturers of electronic navigation equipment either offer, or will be offering, displays that can be seen in an open cockpit with the same clarity as in a nav station belowdecks. Not all of it is affordable yet, but give it a bit of time and it almost certainly will be.

So Where Does That Leave Us?

Distill down all of this technology and what you're left with is an incredible array of easy to use, highly reliable and very capable equipment that can safely get you from place to place with less stress than ever before. Whether you're crossing an ocean or daysailing a bay, at least some of these devices will likely find their way into your cockpit or navigation station.

There are two primary categories of electronic equipment – ship's operations and navigation. Fishing aids are considered by many boat owners to be a crossover group of devices that may eventually win out over the other two types as a result of continuing functional integration. Taken together, these classes of products span the spectrum of current offerings for recreational boaters.

Ship Operations

This group of instruments includes two sub-categories, data displays that present information about current conditions while underway, and those that are integrated into communications devices.

Data Displays

For sailboats, this subgroup includes temperature, speed and depth indicators, as well as the control module for an autopilot. These displays are invariably configured with bright LEDs equipped with backlight control and multiple levels of brightness for night operation.

A powerboat, on the other hand, might use the same autopilot control module as a sailboat if they are using the same make of autopilot. But the powerboat is more likely to use a single multifunction unit for monitoring boat speed and depth, and possibly even water temperature.

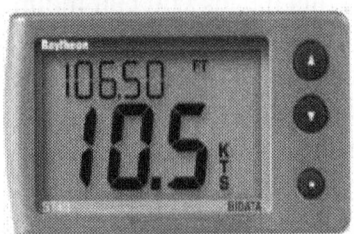

Figure 3-4

Raymarine ST40 speed and depth display

Electronics Aboard -- By Stephen Fishman

In recent years, manufacturers have developed increasingly complex instruments that combine the functionality of several individual instruments. Alternately referred to as bi-data, tri-data or multi-data displays, this class of LED instrument can simultaneously display boat speed and water depth (bi-data) or speed, depth and temperature (tri-data). The catch is that the displays are much smaller than individual displays dedicated to a single function. Multi-data displays are often used as repeaters, visual echoes of a primary instrument, but installed in a location that is remote to the primary. A repeater is often used at a below decks navigation station, at a secondary helm such as a tuna tower, or in a skipper's cabin.

A multi-data display is less expensive to buy than two or three individual devices and requires less space in an already crowded cockpit or helm area. The tradeoff, other than the size of the numbers in the display, is the potential of losing several functions at once if any portion of the device fails and it must be removed for service.

Given the choice, I would opt for dedicated instruments at the helm or in the cockpit, and repeaters in the cabin. If you can afford it, this is the favored tack.

Depending upon the make and model, the LED numerals in these displays can be as small as ½" or as large as 3". Without question, bigger is better. Larger displays let you see a speed or depth readout from anywhere in the cockpit. Aboard a sailboat, this means you can mount these instruments forward of the cockpit across the companionway or on the mast and still easily read the display. Of course, larger displays are proportionally more expensive.

Some instruments in this classification still sport analog displays. Typically, because certain types of data are still best presented with a needle pointing to a reference than with an alphanumeric representation. Two good examples of this exception to the rule are a rudder position indicator for all boats or a wind direction indicator for sailboats. Often, a small LED is used to show wind speed, while an analog display (a needle) indicates the wind direction. Analog displays are typically equipped with the same backlighting and multiple light level controls as their all-electronic cousins.

Communications

Almost without exception, single sideband, marine VHF and ham radios all use a LED display of varying size, depending upon the make, model and type of device.

Figure 3-5

Icom Model 710 single sideband radio

You might choose one model over another because of its power or other features and often, the more elaborate or more expensive radios offer larger displays as part of the high-end package.

Cellular communications and satellite telephones are a special case in that they are a hybrid as regards data display. These devices are normally equipped with LCD displays, as opposed to LED displays, and provide significantly more information than merely a numeric readout.

If you've used a cellular or PCS phone, you know these devices are capable of showing you the date and time and the caller's ID. Some models live a dual existence as telephones and wireless answering machines, while others can connect to the Internet via a cellular modem that is either built-in or installed in a computer.

Electronics Aboard -- By Stephen Fishman

Wireless telephones require LCD displays to show us a lot of information in a small physical space. Earlier in this chapter, I mentioned that LEDs are built in specific sizes but LCDs are displays comprised of hundreds of thousands of pixels. Since each pixel can be activated (turned on or off) individually, the size and shape of the entire display can vary as the need arises. It's this flexibility that has made LCDs the display of choice for so many products.

Navigation

This is by far the largest category of display types, and the group of devices on which manufacturers expend the greatest development effort and budget. It's also the category that has the most rapidly changing and advancing technology. Included in this group are instruments that help direct you safely from one waypoint to another – radar, chartplotters, GPS and DGPS, monitors for PCs and, to a lesser degree, Loran and weather fax. Without question, displays for personal computers and chartplotters are emphasized far beyond the others.

Chartplotters, Fishfinders & More

Depending on the make and model, a chartplotter might incorporate a GPS (or a DGPS in a high-end unit), Wide Area Augmentation System (WAAS) technology, a fishfinder, an incredibly large stable of electronic charts and even radar. This provides the functions of several individual products in one relatively compact unit. A hybrid is significantly higher priced than an individual device but, taken together, represents a significant savings over the purchase of an entire array of dedicated products.

This class of instrument often offers better display technology than its single-purpose cousins since it can be more easily justified by functional integration. Examples of this design philosophy abound in products such as Simrad's CA40.

Electronics Aboard -- By *Stephen Fishman*

This is a multifunction navigation tool that integrates radar, a differential GPS, chartplotting and a fishfinder all in one unit equipped with an LCD color display.

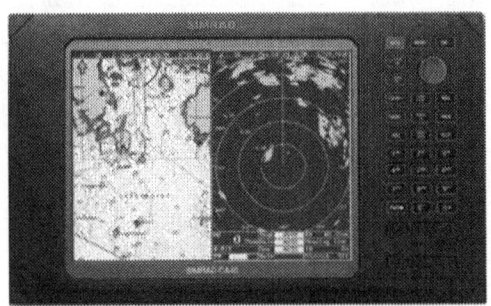

Figure 3-6

Simrad CA-40 radar/chartplotter

This bright 14-inch display offers a user-selectable range of display options, including multiple shades of red for night use at a darkened helm. In addition, it has a sharp, split-screen option that pairs an overhead radar view with a topographic chart of the same area. A less expensive model is also available that sports a 10-inch display, a good choice if you want all the integration but have less real estate available at the helm or in a nav area below.

Simrad is by no means alone in this design category. Raytheon, Furuno, Garmin and many others offer at least one model capable of showing you simultaneous multiple functions. These include a depth image and a traditional chart view, a radar image overlaying a chart, or a fishfinder image beside a view of bottom topography in two-dimensions.

Many of these combination products sport monochrome displays instead of color. As a result, they provide a more affordable way to take advantage of all this wonderful technology without having to sell the boat to do it.

Typically, integrated navigation electronics with monochrome displays don't include radar. This helps to maintain a price point the average boater can afford. Besides,

Electronics Aboard -- By Stephen Fishman

sales of radar systems are very small, relative to sales of fishfinders, chartplotters and GPS units, and for good reason. The vast majority of us are fair-weather sailors who never leave our home waters or avoid situations that might place us and our vessels in peril. As far as I'm concerned, that's the way it should be. After all, most of us are engineers, managers or marketing people who love the water and want to have fun when we take to our boats.

Size Matters

Although mentioned only in passing, it's a good idea to pay close attention to the overall size of the product and not just the size of the display. A chartplotter may have a 10.4-inch display but it might have overall dimensions of 10 inches x 16 inches. An LCD display of 15 inches might be mounted in a case that consumes as much as 1-1/2 square feet of helm area.

Screen displays for marine navigation systems are measured in the same way as the televisions in our homes. This means the measurement is taken diagonally across the screen and, with some exceptions, relates to the viewable area of the screen. Although CRT displays are typically square like most televisions and traditional computer monitors, LCD marine displays are almost universally rectangular in shape. A 15 inch LCD display on a chartplotter, fishfinder or radar won't look as large as the same screen specification for a color CRT.

"Dumb" Displays

Monitors are significantly different than displays in integrated navigation systems. Monitor screens tend to be larger, higher in resolution, capable of reproducing vastly more colors and, given the features, a generally better value. This is not to say these displays are cheap, by any stretch they'll still cost you a pretty penny. Considering what you get for what you spend, this alternative may be worth considering.

Electronics Aboard -- By Stephen Fishman

Although some displays are CRTs that look like high-definition television sets, most marine terminal displays are LCD screens. They range in price from a few hundred to several thousands of dollars. Virtually all of these devices are intended for flush-mount installations. Meaning they are made to be set into the face of a helm or navigation area. Some of these displays have accessory mounts that allow them to be installed on top of a hard surface or hung from a rigid overhead support.

With few exceptions, LCD displays have two properties in common, regardless of other features – they must be connected to a personal computer and they are sealed against the weather to one degree or another. Let's take the second point first.

Built To Take It

It's impossible to spend much time strolling down the aisles of a local chandlery without coming across the words "harsh marine environment." It is this phrase that drives marine equipment manufacturers to create products that will stand up against the worst that the sea has to offer. Nowhere is this more evident than in marine electronics, with screen displays being one of the best examples.

The current crop of LCD computer displays are constructed with O-rings between sections of the casing to help prevent salt and moisture entry. They have pocket buttons or integrated membrane covers that prevent water entry on the keypad. Computer connections are complex fittings that are keyed to fit only one way, seal out moisture with locking rings and often have gold contacts. The display itself is typically sealed within the case with multiple layers of high-tech gaskets and adhesives. Some of these displays are built so well they're used by the military.

Electronics Aboard -- By Stephen Fishman

What You See

Okay, so what exactly does this mean to you and me? How do we compare one technically complex product with another? Well, a bit of techno-babble might be just the thing to give you an idea of just how much design effort is put into these displays:

High-nit and high aperture refers to the brightness of the image. A higher number generally means a brighter screen, but there appears to be no standard measurement method, so this number alone can be misleading.

Backlighting helps the image stand out visually from the background of the screen "base". Backlighting is usually adjustable and, taken together with a high "nit" rating can provide an idea about how well the display can be seen in sunlight.

Enhanced light guide technology produces a more even brightness across the entire display.

Index matching film helps assure that contrast between different colors is as optimal as possible.

Anti-glare and anti-reflection coatings are absolutely necessary to minimize glare and reflections from water, stainless steel and other sources.

There are three other significant technical aspects of displays that you should know about – angle of view, color range and resolution. Angle of view determines how far off-center you can be and still readily see the entire display. Typically, the higher the number the better, with the goal being a viewing angle of 135 degrees or more. The best displays offer viewing angles of up to 165 degrees. This isn't much of a consideration if you're standing at the helm and the display is hanging from an overhead strut right in front of you. But if you're on a sailboat at 20 degrees of heel and standing to the side of the wheel bracing yourself in the corner of the cockpit, a wide angle of heel may have a different reality.

Electronics Aboard -- By Stephen Fishman

Figure 3-7

PinPoint Systems LCD marine displays

Another important technical rating is the number of colors that can be displayed. If the monitor is a 16-bit display, it should have a range of 65 thousand colors. A 24-bit display should be capable of 65 million colors. The latter is probably the same specification as the monitor on your computer at the office. Compared to displays integrated into chartplotters and fishfinders that can display only 16 colors, independent displays offer a substantially different view of charting and navigation.

The third technical spec, resolution, tends to have more significance in large LCD displays than it does for small displays built into standalone devices. An expensive high-end chartplotter might have a color display capable of 640x480 resolution (basic VGA resolution), but dedicated LCD marine displays start at this point and go far beyond.

It's not unusual for an LCD display to have 800x600 super VGA resolution on a 12-inch display, and some real high-end displays are now being built with 1024x768 X-VGA resolution on a 15-inch display.

Electronics Aboard -- By Stephen Fishman

Figure 3-8

Flat screen LCD on a flybridge

Within the confines of a cockpit, flybridge or nav area in the cabin, a 15-inch display is like watching wide-screen high-definition television.

Sticker Shock

I have intentionally avoided price discussions throughout this book because pricing and models change so frequently and it's your opinion not mine. What is outrageous to one person might seem reasonable to another. But it might be wise to put things in perspective regarding dedicated computer displays.

As an example, the owner of a 40-foot Island Gypsy trawler might invest $3,500 in a radar, or the skipper of a 42-foot Catalina sailboat might spend $2,000, or more, on a DGPS/chartplotter. Most boaters wouldn't consider these expenditures to be excessive. But an LCD marine display might set you back $2,000 to $4,000, and that's without the computer.

Electronics Aboard -- *By Stephen Fishman*

Dedicated displays are not for everyone but, that said, one of the greatest certainties of the modern world is that technology always gets cheaper. In my experience, the time continues to shorten between the high-cost introduction of an electronic product and its general usage price.

It's my guess that, in the not-too-distant future, we'll all be able to install bright, high-resolution daylight-viewable displays for a fraction of their current price. Personally, I can't wait.

Electronics Aboard -- By Stephen Fishman

Electronics Aboard -- By Stephen Fishman

Chapter Four
VHF Marine Radios

Officially termed a "VHF-FM marine radiotelephone," a very high frequency (VHF) radio is still the most widely used means of electronic communication across the water. The VHF frequency band extends from 30 to 300 MHz but, as recreational boaters, we're only concerned with the portion of the band between 156 and 163 MHz.

Notice that I specified "electronic" communication because there are also low-tech methods of communication that have been around for centuries, some of which are still used today.

The practice of hoisting a series of flags to convey a message can be traced back almost as far as sailing itself. Signaling with an intermittent light source is nearly as old as a means of stringing together a group of letters, words or phrases. Somewhere along the way, flares and smoke signals were developed, along with sounds such as a bell or horn, in an effort to provide better ways of broadcasting a warning or cry for help. At the time of their introduction, these devices were thought of as the newest and best ways of communicating on the water.

In the high-tech world of electronics, there are a myriad of ways to get someone's attention electronically, other than by using a marine VHF radio. These include a ham radio, single sideband, satellite telephone, and even email, to name a few.

Interestingly, in June, 1996, the U.S. Federal Communications Commission made a decision to suspend the

Electronics Aboard -- *By Stephen Fishman*

requirement in U.S. waters that every boat under 65-feet with a marine VHF radio also had to have a ship's station license. If you received a license prior to June, 1996, the call letters can still be used if you like. Today, only the vessel name is required at the beginning and end of a transmission. All of the other FCC-mandated marine radio rules are still in effect, but most of the regulations pertain to commercial and military vessels.

It's also interesting to note that the FCC retains the right to reverse the suspension ruling if other rules for marine radio broadcasting aren't followed. If the suspension ruling is rescinded in the future, mandatory licensing could once again be the law. It wasn't a big deal in the past - a simple form and a nominal one-time fee - but it might be a big deal if the FCC ever gets the feeling that VHF radio usage has become too unruly.

By the way, if you decide to sail to a foreign country, you ARE required by the FCC to have a ship's station license in addition to other licenses for equipment, such as a ham radio or a single sideband.

A Word Of Warning

Using a VHF radio on the water is just about the same as using a CB radio on land, and it carries the same problem when used. There is no privacy. I repeat. There is NO privacy when you are speaking on a VHF marine band radio. It's like talking on a huge party line.

If you don't know what a party line is, it means that everyone who is tuned in can hear every word you say. No special devices. No "bugs." No nothing. All anyone has to do is turn on the VHF radio and listen to channel 16, or whatever channel they think is being used.

You wouldn't believe some of the private things people say when they forget that it's not like talking on the telephone.

Stories abound of people making dates, discussing the activities of the night before, trading stories of illnesses and exchanging opinions about co-workers or supervisors. They

Electronics Aboard -- By Stephen Fishman

have even been known to cuss and scream when their boat malfunctions, while blaming everyone but themselves for their troubles. It's usually not a pleasant sight and it's nearly always too much information.

I Want One Because...

In coastal areas, a failed engine, dead bilge pump or a fast-approaching storm are all reasons why you should have a marine VHF radio on board. The United States Coast Guard monitors marine VHF bands 24-hours a day, seven days a week. If a real emergency arises, someone who can help you is standing by. In addition, many towing and rescue services monitor VHF, and most have the means to locate your boat by homing in on your VHF signal.

A VHF radio can also provide access to waterborne conveniences such as supplies and fuel delivery, reservations at restaurants and marinas, boating operations such as a drawbridge or even just chatting with people aboard other vessels.

Remember

The signal from a VHF radio is essentially a line-of-sight communication. Across the water, this translates to a broadcast range of about twenty nautical miles, although some sources suggest that fifteen miles is a more realistic transmission limit. This distance limitation is primarily due to the earth's curvature, but the distance can be extended quite a bit under some circumstances. For example, if there is significant cloud cover or a low ceiling of clouds, the signal can "bounce" back to the surface, effectively extending the range by as much as 50% further than normal. Under very unusual conditions, a VHF radio signal can be heard as far away as 200 miles when a "duct" is formed between the earth and an air layer. This air layer is at several thousand feet and warmer than the surface, instead of cooler.

Electronics Aboard -- By Stephen Fishman

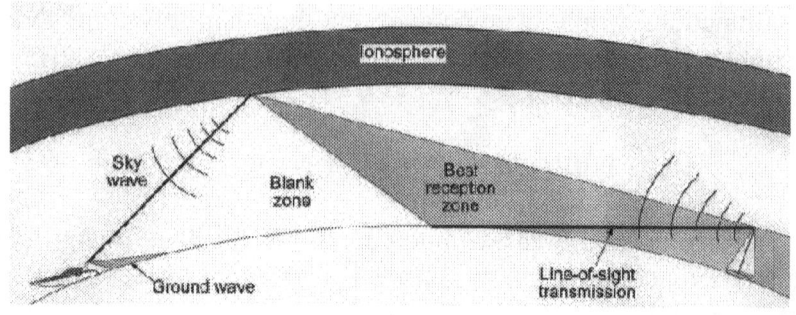

Figure 4-1

VHF radio broadcast

By design, VHF radio communication is effectively restricted to coastal areas and areas with a high boating population.

While fifteen or twenty miles is the nominal limit for ship-to-ship communications, this distance can be expected to double when broadcasting ship-to-shore. This is because land-based antennas are built much taller than those on boats, which brings us to the next thing that affects the distance of a VHF broadcast - the antenna.

You Gotta Have A Good One

Without an antenna, a marine VHF radio can't perform the task for which it was designed. In fact, trying to operate a radio without an antenna can often lead to a "blowout" of the device because the signal has nowhere to go.

Without exception, the higher the antenna the greater the distance the signal will travel. This means a sailboat will have a longer broadcast range than a powerboat since VHF antennas on sailboats are mounted at the top of the mast. This height differential is greater on smaller boats and lessens as vessel length increases due to taller deck structures such as a flybridge or tuna tower.

Although antenna height and weather conditions are the primary factors affecting transmission distance, the power of the radio – expressed in watts – also contributes to overall performance.

The Power

In the same way that notebook computers are less powerful than their desktop cousins, handheld VHF radios are less powerful than physically larger, permanently mounted units. While handheld units can be rated as high as 6 watts or as low as 3 watts, a typical handheld VHF radio has 5 watts of power.

Figure 4-2

Fixed-mount VHF radio

By comparison, most fixed-mount VHF radios are rated at 25 watts. It doesn't take much imagination to expect a 25-watt radio to have more power than a 5-watt model. However, this is not so much an accurate measurement of radio performance as it is just another factor affecting a radio's transmission capabilities.

Note: *25-watts is the maximum power currently allowed by the FCC for marine VHF radios.*

Electronics Aboard -- By Stephen Fishman

The Difference

Allowing for the difference in power ratings and whether they are handheld or fixed-mount units, most marine VHF radios have many features in common, including:

- A button that immediately accesses channel 16
- All U.S. channels are built-in
- International channels
- Weather channels
- A channel selector – button/knob
- Current channel indicator or display
- On/Off switch
- Microphone "key" switch
- A one-watt switch for close range transmissions
- A DSC "panic" button on newer models

Although most VHF radios are created equal, there are some distinct differences between handheld and fixed mount units, irrespective of price. For example, most handheld radios are built in such a way that they can be dropped into the water and still be expected to work when retrieved, without damage to their electronics or rechargeable batteries.

Nearly all fixed-mount radios can scan the entire range of available channels instead of only a few pre-selected channels, and most have all-aluminum housings. As previously mentioned, fixed-mounts are more powerful.

Another common feature of most fixed-mount VHF radios is the ability to hail another vessel or someone in the water by means of a "bullhorn." A "horn" can be a very effective way of getting the attention of someone nearby.

If you can afford only one type of radio, a handheld or a fixed-mount, I suggest a fixed-mount every time. If you can afford both, consider owning one of each type if for, no other reason than, peace of mind. You can never have too many backups.

Electronics Aboard -- By Stephen Fishman

You May Want Both

Other than portability, handheld radios offer something else worth noting - they do not rely upon the vessel's power. At first blush this may seem redundant but consider losing all ship's power with only a fix-mount VHF.

Figure 4-3

Handheld VHF radio

This is not far-fetched. Every towing service I have spoken with agreed that dead batteries are the single, most common reason for a boater to request assistance.

Where Do I Mount It?

Depending upon the vessel, VHF radios can be found in the cabin, on the flybridge or in the cockpit. Regardless of the location, two issues are paramount – protection from the weather and instant access.

To be of value, a radio should be installed close to where you normally operate the boat so it's within east reach. The location might be at an interior helm, at the top of a tuna tower or at the aft end of a T-shaped cockpit. It is worth little if you are forced to leave the wheel to use it, especially if you regularly singlehand your boat. This caveat might seem simplistic, but you would surprised to discover how many people install a VHF radio in a place that looks great but offers no practical value.

Most of the current crop of marine electronics are water-resistant at a minimum and waterproof at best. While not all marine instruments are ready for the exposure of the cockpit, virtually all models can be installed in an enclosure that protects the radio from direct sun and spray. Most fixed-mount models can be installed using a bracket included with the radio, resulting in a quick and inexpensive method of installation.

Figure 4-4

Flush-mount

You'll have a cleaner, more professional installation, however, if you use a faceplate or trim plate to flush-mount the radio. Recess the radio so only the control panel and microphone protrude above the surface. Cutting a large rectangular hole into the surface of the helm station or cockpit coaming can be a scary prospect if you've never done it before. If you're reluctant to do this yourself, a marine contractor can help. When it comes to cutting big holes in people's boats, contractors have no fear.

Protocol

Recreational boaters typically use only a handful of channels for communication with other boaters or with land-based facilities. Many channels are set aside for commercial use, some are used by the military and other channels are reserved for use within the confines of a single large vessel,

Electronics Aboard -- By Stephen Fishman

such as a cruise ship.

Still, there are several channels available for noncommercial use and they are divided into roughly three types; calling and emergency channels, weather channels and "chat" channels. Experienced boaters are aware of the use for each type and use them accordingly. Inconsiderate boaters don't use a marine VHF radio as a private telephone for long without retribution from fellow mariners.

The correct way to open and close a conversation on a VHF radio is to say the vessel name - twice at the beginning and once at the end of a transmission.

For example, for many years my wife, Deborah, and I lived aboard a sailboat named *Lady Greyhawke*. *Mal De Mer* was a beautiful forty-six foot traditional schooner owned by friends of ours who lived aboard in a different marina. For us, a typical opening call was "Lady Greyhawke, Lady Greyhawke calling Mal De Mer, Lady Greyhawke calling Mal De Mer. Over." When the conversation was through, a typical sign-off for us was "Lady Greyhawke out" or, if we were out on the water at the time, "Lady Greyhawke clear and monitoring 16."

Sometimes, part of the reason a name is chosen for a vessel is because of how it will sound when using a VHF radio. For example, one friend of ours lives aboard a thirty-five foot sailboat named *Promises*. His calls to us always bring a smile when he opens a VHF transmission by saying "Promises, Promises." Another boater we know owns a thirty-foot performance boat he intentionally named "Hubba"

If you remember nothing else, bear in mind that channel 16 and channel 9 are to be used for "hailing or distress" only. The Coast Guard takes a very dim view of boaters who want to make dinner reservations while on channel 16. Actually, it's a felony to interfere with emergency traffic, not to mention lives may be at stake.

You will influence friends and enemies alike – and keep the authorities off your back - if you "call" on channel 16 or channel 9 and then move your conversation to a different channel.

Electronics Aboard -- By Stephen Fishman

Recreational Channels

Channel	Recommended FCC Use
6	Ship-to-ship safety warnings (also called *Securite'*)
9	Hailing - Ship-to-ship and coast-to-coast calling to commercial docks, marinas, and some clubs). This one is also used as an alternate calling channel. Used at some locks and bridges. **Note:** *Channel 09 is often used by the bridge tenders. If the bridge tender does not answer on 09, use the ship's horn to sound one long and one short blast to signal your intent to pass under the bridge when opened. This signal can be repeated as often as needed*
13	Ship-to-ship navigation
16	Hailing, safety and distress. Channel 16 is for CALLING and EMERGENCY use only! U.S. Coast Guard information broadcasts. Used for emergency communication after being told by the Coast Guard to change from another channel
24-28	Marine operator connection to land-based line
67	Commercial ships
68-69	Non-commercial ship-to-ship and ship-to-shore communication
70	Distress and safety calling for Digital Selective Calling (DSC) only*
71	Non-commercial ship-to-ship and ship-to-shore
72	Non-commercial ship-to-ship communication only
78A	Non-commercial ship-to-ship and ship-to-shore communication
84-88	Marine operator connection to land-based line

* Digital Selective Calling (DSC) is like having a "panic button." When DSC is activated, an encoded distress signal is automatically broadcast that can be received by nearby vessels with DSC-equipped radios. If the radio has been connected to a Loran or GPS (Global Positioning System), the transmission will include the location of the broadcast.

Electronics Aboard -- By Stephen Fishman

All marine VHF radiotelephones have the channels listed above The chart lists the channels available for conversation, communication and radio checks. If a channel number is not listed in the chart, it means that the channel is not available for public or noncommercial use. It would be best to avoid attempting to access it even if your radio displays the number.

Similar to the signal-to-noise ratio specification in audio equipment, selectivity is a measurement of how well the radio isolates a selected channel from other adjacent channels. This is expressed in decibels. This designation is often noted as a negative number, but the highest number possible is always best, i.e.; -45dB is better than -55dB.

The FCC has mandated that by 1999, all new fixed-mount marine VHF radios have to be equipped with DSC.

Antennas & Signal Strength

As mentioned earlier in this chapter, a VHF radio transmission is a line-of-sight transmission that relies heavily on an unobstructed view of the target receiver. There are two fundamental ways to boost the sending and receiving range of a VHF signal – increasing the height of the antenna above the surface and increasing the gain.

Gain is a relative rating in decibels (dB) that represents the ability of your antenna to amplify signals, both incoming and outgoing. Gain increases the power of the signal exponentially, which means even a small increase can make a significant difference. An increase in gain of 3dB will effectively double the strength of the signal, while an increase of 6dB will quadruple it. As you might guess, the higher the gain, the better.

As the gain increases, the beam becomes more focused. This can cause a "fading" of the signal on a rolling sea. A focused signal must be aimed more precisely and must be more stable to be effective. The best increases in gain will result from a narrowing beam on a fixed, land-based platform.

Electronics Aboard -- By Stephen Fishman

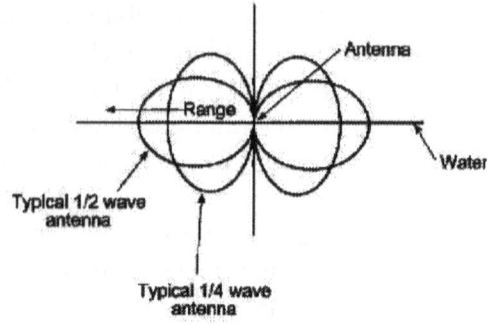

Figure 4-5

Wavelength range

The figure shows the radiation pattern of two different antennas. Note the quarter wavelength antenna has the highest angle of radiation but it also has the lowest gain. The half wavelength antenna has both a lower angle of radiation and a higher gain, giving it superior performance at sea level. All other factors being equal, choosing an antenna with a longer wavelength results in an increased transmission distance.

A notable exception to this axiom is an antenna mounted at the top of a sailboat mast. On our typical 35-foot sailboat, the masthead can easily be fifty feet above the surface. At that height, even a moderate gain antenna will yield a greatly increased range over using the same antenna on a motoryacht's flybridge arch, twenty feet off the water.

A common marine VHF antenna is eight feet long and has a gain of either 3dB or 6dB, with a maximum power handling capacity of 50 watts. There are a few antennas available up to fourteen feet in length that offer a gain of 8dB or 9dB, and have the ability to handle up to 200 watts of power.

What happens when you try to jam too much power into antenna designed for much less? Anything from blowing the capacitor in the antenna to feeding power back into the radio and frying the circuits of the radio.

Electronics Aboard -- By Stephen Fishman

Near shore, stainless steel whip antennas are often preferred due to their compact size and lower cost and are the hands-down choice for the top of a mast. Higher gain antennas are typically made of fiberglass, or a combination of a fiberglass shaft topped with a stainless steel whip. Skimming any marine catalogue will quickly reveal that fiberglass antennas are more costly, require robust mounts and longer, heavier cables.

Cables & Such

Antenna cable is a coax type cable not much different from what your local television cable service uses. Called RG-58 or RG-8X, these cables are PVC-coated and usually 25 feet of cable is pre-attached to the antenna.

If you feel there is more cable than you need, DO NOT cut the cable. It will create headaches for you including corrosion, loss of signal strength, and interference with the radio's ground. Instead, excess cable should be coiled in large loops and stored in a place as far away as possible from other electronic devices. If you can, keep the cable run to 25-feet or less, and avoid placing kinks or sharp bends in the cable when snaking it through the boat.

For runs longer than 25-feet, a low-loss, non-marine cable such as RG-8, RG-8U or RG-213, should be used. But beware, these cables may provide the distance you need but they're insulated with a foam-filler that can trap moisture, resulting in accelerated internal corrosion and a degraded signal. If you must make a run longer than 25-feet, use an extension that fulfills three basic requirements:

- No longer than 25-feet in length
- Matches the original PVC-coated antenna cable
- Uses marine-grade connectors

By the way, an antenna should not be mounted closer than three feet to most marine VHF radios. As the power output of the radio increases, so does the minimum antenna distance from the radio.

The Connection

The connection between the antenna cable and the antenna, as well as connectors between spliced sections of cable, should be made using only PL-259 connectors. To help prevent corrosion problems, spray the connectors with a silicone protectant such as Corrosion Block®, or wrap each connection with heat shrink tubing or rigging tape.

If it becomes necessary to repair a PVC-coated antenna cable, cut the cable cleanly across its diameter using a sharp knife or proper wire cutters. Replace the PL-259 connector with either a solderless crimp-on replacement, or use 60/40 rosin core solder and a soldering iron of at least 300 watts.

At The Bottom

The fitting that threads into the base of the antenna mount is called a ferule. This fitting is often made of nylon or plastic, and that's great for small boats or light near-shore use. If you like to go offshore fishing or if you race your boat, you might consider a metal ferule. These activities will cause the antenna to flex more violently, putting a strain on the mount.

When replacing a ferule it is critical the materials match. A plastic ferule should be used with a plastic or nylon antenna mount, and a stainless steel ferule should be used with a stainless or chrome-plated antenna mount.

Always Remember

A marine VHF radio is a huge party line. When you move to a new channel, take a moment to monitor the channel before you begin speaking. By doing so you'll know if someone else is currently using it for other two-way

Electronics Aboard -- By Stephen Fishman

communications. If your radio has dual or triple scan capability, a good practice is to monitor the channel you would like to use prior to calling. Don't forget to use a low power (1 watt) setting whenever possible. A high power broadcast can damage the receiving radio, as well as the ears of the person on the other end of the transmission.

I can't stress this one issue enough: Whatever you say over the airwaves will be heard by everyone in range and monitoring the channel. Be careful what you say.

Parents take note. If there are children on board, make sure they know your VHF radio is not a karaoke microphone.

Electronics Aboard -- By Stephen Fishman

Electronics Aboard -- By Stephen Fishman

Chapter Five
Fishfinders

If you like to fish, you have two basic choices – think of some way to get the fish to come to you, or go out there and find them. I don't know about you, but I've never been very good at waiting, especially when it comes to something unlikely to happen.

A Neat Gadget

Fishfinders are a depth sounder on steroids. Essentially, sonar technology put to use for something a bit more laid back than hunting military targets. A fishfinder is an echo sounder comprised of two components, a transducer and an image display.

The fishfinder converts electrical energy into electronic pulses and sends the pulses to a transducer mounted below the waterline. The transducer converts the electronic pulses into ultrasonic sound waves that travel through the water at a speed of about 4,800 feet per second, or about 3,200 miles an hour.

Sound waves travel much faster through water than through air, where their top speed is only 1,100 feet per second, or about 750 miles per hour.

The sound waves bounce off the bottom – echo – and are picked up by the transducer. The transducer converts the sound waves back to electrical impulses and sends them back to the fishfinder. The data is displayed on a CRT or LCD screen. The images seen on the display are the result of a calculation that determines how much time elapsed between the transmission the returning echo.

The Keys To Success

Before you can locate the fish, you have to properly locate the transducer.

There are two types of transducers – transom-mounted and through-hull mounted. Both types work best when flush with the bottom of the hull, and located away from prop turbulence and other water-induced disturbances.

Transducers require regular cleaning with a fine (240-grit) sandpaper, bronze wool or an abrasive pad such as a 3M® Scotch-Brite pad. The transducer face should be painted with a marine growth inhibitor, but NEVER use bottom paint as it will interfere with the effectiveness of the transducer signal.

Of the two types, a transom-mounted transducer is preferred, and for some very practical reasons.

First, it's a lot less expensive to bolt a transducer to the transom than it is to haul the boat and cut a hole in the hull. Some sailors have likened the practice to skydiving: why would anyone want to jump out of a perfectly good airplane? Similarly, why would anyone want to put a large hole in the bottom of the boat when there are easier and less expensive alternatives?

Figure 5-1

Transom transducer

Electronics Aboard -- *By Stephen Fishman*

A transom-mounted transducer is installed on the transom. Although it can be physically installed on any boat, it's best use is on boats with outboard motors, including sailboats. Transom-mounted transducers offer three distinct advantages over through-hull transducers:

- They're easier to clean and maintain because their location is so accessible
- They can be more readily changed out if a replacement is needed or if you want to update your system
- Almost anyone handy with tools can install one

There are, however, two caveats to bear in mind if you decide to install a transom-mounted transducer. First, make sure the face of the transducer is submerged even when the boat is in the slip - but *only* the face. The tough part is to strike a balance between making sure the face is always wet and, at the same time, not too far beneath the surface of the hull.

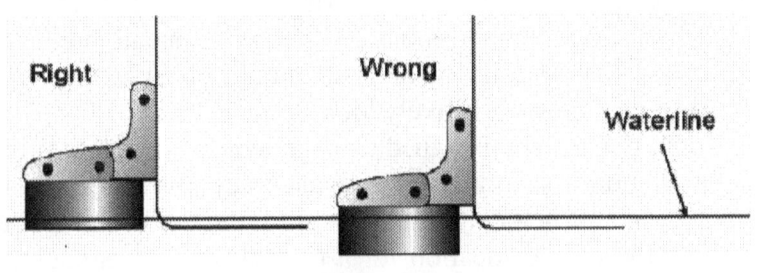

Figure 5-2

Wet but not too deep

The second point to remember is the location of the transducer should always be away from through-hull fittings, a motor mount or anything else that might cause turbulence. Ideally, the water flowing across the face of a transducer should leave a trail that is free of bubbles and as little wake as possible.

A through-hull transducer can be mounted in any hull

regardless of its shape, but it's critical to consider where along the centerline the transducer should be located. For example, the best place to install a transducer on a planing hull is far aft, in a flat area that will remain submerged even when the boat gets up on a plane.

Figure 5-3

Through-hull transducer

On curved hulls, such as those of most sailboats, a fairing block is often needed in order to orient the transducer as straight down as possible. Although a small angle off vertical is okay, a sailboat skipper should consider motoring instead of sailing when actively looking for fish.

A through-hull transducer generally yields the best results in both performance and accuracy over a transom-mounted unit. Whether you have a slow boat or a show boat, choosing the proper location for a transducer is paramount. A transducer will perform best when located in the most advantageous place relative to hull curvature and keel arrangements.

As shown in Figure 5-4, correct transducer placement has a lot to do with the type of hull (planing or displacement) and the type of keel. Like transom-mounted transducers, through-hull units should be installed in a place as free as possible from turbulence.

If you're the one who cuts out the hole and installs the transducer, don't be stingy with the bedding compound. Apply it generously both internally and on the outside of the hull. You can always trim away the excess, but the last thing you want to do is haul the boat to fix a leak.

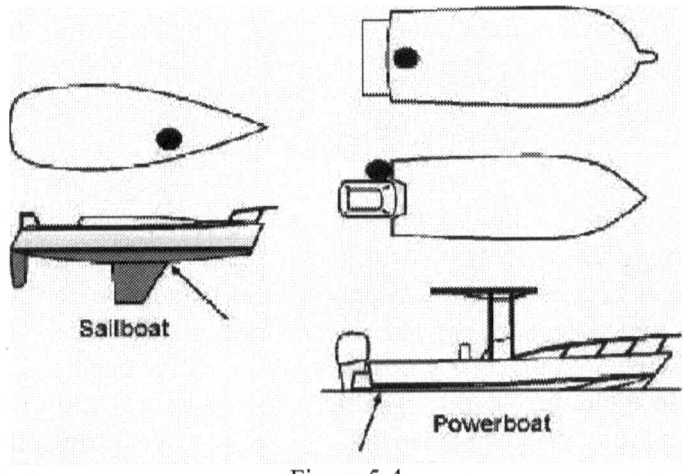

Figure 5-4

Various transducer locations

Occasionally, you will come across a "shoot-through" transducer. This type is rather rare since it only works well with solid fiberglass hulls. This leaves out most modern sport boats and sailboats since these tend to be made with foam flotation between layers of fiberglass.

As the name implies, a shoot-through looks at the bottom from inside the boat, sending its soundings through the hull instead of directly into the water. This type of transducer can perform nearly as well as a through-hull type, but the installation must satisfy two requirements:

• It must be as precisely vertical as possible
• The transducer's surface next to the hull's interior must be completely submerged in silicone or the material supplied with the unit

Note: *There can be absolutely no air bubbles between the transducer and the hull.*

Electronics Aboard -- By Stephen Fishman

A shoot-through transducer can be epoxied to the inside of the hull or it can be set into a glob of silicone. Some models are designed to be bolted down, while others are installed inside an enclosure filled with oil. Remember to aim the transducer so it is as close to vertical as possible.

Which Transducer?

Some fishfinders offer inputs in addition to a sounding transceiver/transducer. Additional sensors can provide temperature and boat speed data. These accessory transducers are mounted separately from the fishfinder's sounder.

Temperature and speed sensors are available in both transom-mounted or through-hull versions. These are installed with the same considerations for operation. Some manufacturers have recently begun offering "multi-sensors" that combine all three functions in one transducer housing, but most of these systems are still rather costly. As you might expect of any integrated system, if one part of a multi-sensor malfunctions, the entire array must be removed for repair.

Cables

I have yet to see a fishfinder installation in which there wasn't a zillion miles of leftover cable. Whatever you do, don't cut the cable and try to splice it. Coil all the extra cable in a nice, out of the way place and forget about it. I know of several skippers who took issue with this due to their insistence on spelling "anal-retentive" with a hyphen. In each instance, the accuracy of the fishfinder was degraded and in one case the cable had to be replaced.

If you need a longer cable, which is rare on most pleasure craft, additional lengths of cable are available through your local marine supplier.

Electronics Aboard -- By Stephen Fishman

Depth Range

Many newer models of fishfinders have a dual range control that makes them more useful in deeper water. Most of us fish in relatively shallow water, often no deeper than 100 feet, but sportfishing game can often exceed a half mile in depth.

Figure 5-5

Commercial grade fishfinder

For shallower targets, a high-frequency (HF) setting of 200 kHz is best. This frequency is useful for fish such as mackerel that have no swim bladder, as well as for more readily discriminating between schools of small fish and a single large one on a display.

Conversely, a low-frequency (LF) setting of 50 kHz is better for deep-water targets and provides better sea bottom discrimination. Low frequencies are also quite useful for selecting individual big fish at 4,000 feet, or more. A dual-range fishfinder provides the best of two worlds – high-definition displays from moderate depths as well as the ability to sound to significant depths.

Electronics Aboard -- By Stephen Fishman

Displays

Echo information from a transducer is displayed either as a color image of up to sixteen colors, or as a monochrome gray scale image. The stronger the returning echo, the brighter the object appears on the screen. With luck, the picture will include images of fish along with bottom contours.

A monochrome display on most fishfinders shows everything in eight shades of gray. Strong signals, such as reflections from a hard bottom, show up as very dark shades, while debris or individual fish are seen as lighter grays. Schools of fish are rendered as something akin to a floating cloud.

A color display is a wonderful X-ray of the underwater world, showing strong echoes in reds, yellows and oranges depending on the relative intensity of the return signal. Weaker signals show up as greens and the weakest echoes as blues. If you've ever seen a rainbow, you'll be familiar with this progression of colors across the spectrum. Depending on the make and model, a color fishfinder displays either eight colors or sixteen colors.

Schools of baitfish and pods of other small fish are usually seen as blue-green, while dense concentrations of forage fish, especially larger versions, pass the green range and approach the yellow representation.

Individual gamefish are likely to display as yellow, but as they grow larger in size and number, they can easily scoot right through yellow and orange to red.

Structures on the sea floor, such as shipwrecks and artificial reefs, are usually a dark orange or red. In a similar fashion, natural projections such as rock piles and other outcroppings can often be recognized by their dark, warm colors.

When all of these varied elements are mixed together, your display might be a broad spectrum of colors with a pale blue-green cloud of baitfish, yellow and orange moving marks on the sides and a dark red background to the entire scene.

Electronics Aboard -- By Stephen Fishman

Soft bottom topography, such as mud or grass, is usually displayed as a thin red line. Harder bottom material such as sand, rock or clay typically appears as a thick, dark red line. In general, a thicker, harder bottom will produce a thicker, darker line.

The two basic types of fishfinder displays are cathode ray tube (CRT) and liquid crystal display (LCD). The CRT type is similar to television in that it uses a vacuum tube. The image on a CRT is easy to see in normal or dimmed light but increasingly difficult to see as the ambient light brightens, as would be the case on a flybridge or in an open cockpit.

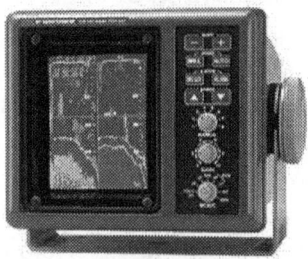

Figure 5-6

Color CRT display

Unlike CRTs for devices such as radar, most fishfinder CRTs are available in color and can display up to sixteen colors. The disadvantage of a CRT is it needs to be shielded from the elements, which is just as well since it works better inside the cabin anyway.

An LCD display, on the other hand, usually has a larger image area and can be more easily seen in sunlight, whether the screen is a backlit or front-lit display. An LCD screen is similar to the new flat screen displays found on personal computers. Like an LCD made for a PC, the resolution is not as high as a CRT but the display is usually in color, making it easier to distinguish between various contours and underwater objects.

Electronics Aboard -- By Stephen Fishman

Figure 5-7

LCD flat color display

Most LCD displays are either weather-resistant or waterproof, depending upon the make and model. You can't exactly throw the screen in the water and still expect it to work, but most of them will survive misty rain, fog or the occasional wave.

There are two notable exceptions to the general rule about resolution. In recent years, TFT technology has been integrated into fishfinder displays, yielding a much higher-resolution display. This is the same technology now used on notebook computer screens to provide a bright, sharp flat screen display that is very thin. For fishfinders, however, the screen size is usually limited to something about five- or six-inches wide and ten-inches tall.

The other exception is the increased use of marinized personal computer flat screen displays. These are VGA, non-interlaced displays, providing the same resolution and screen size you would expect to see if the screen was connected to a PC. Although the display resolution is 640 x 480 pixels, the number of colors is still limited to either eight or sixteen.

Power Consumption

Like the multiple range option of either LF or HF, depending on the depth in which you're fishing, most fishfinders also have more than one power output setting.

Electronics Aboard -- By *Stephen Fishman*

Fishfinders typically have at least two power output settings, providing more power for deep water, low-frequency applications. The settings range from a low of 350 watts to a high-power option of 3,000 watts.

On powerboats, the power consumption rating of a fishfinder is of little consequence since the engine runs constantly. Even on a sailboat, running the engine makes a lot of sense when using the fishfinder because it yields greater accuracy due to a reduced angle of heel. For these reasons, skippers of any type of vessel are rarely concerned about power consumption.

In addition to dual frequency ranges, multiple power output options and a choice of displays, most fishfinders also offer these features:

- A zoom function to isolate and magnify a portion of the screen
- A choice of feet, fathoms or metric measurement display
- Alarms that can be set to a predetermined depth
- On-screen operation and set up menus
- NMEA0183 interface capability for connection to other electronic devices
- Installation options that include overhead, surface-mounting or flush-mounting

As always, the more you're willing to spend, the more you'll find in the way of options, controls and accessories. But, unlike other electronic marine devices, a fishfinder gives you the chance of taking home more than just a story.

Electronics Aboard -- By Stephen Fishman

Electronics Aboard -- By Stephen Fishman

Chapter Six
Electronic Charting

Even to the casual observer, it's easy to see computers are not only here to stay but have become an integral part of our daily lives. In one way or another, we use computers everyday – all day - to help cook our food, entertain us, or make our automobiles more efficient and reliable. Computers help provide public services from, police and fire response, to food stamps and welfare payments. Cell telephones were impossible without computer technology and who isn't familiar with cable TV receivers, satellite dishes and wireless Internet connections?

How heavily you rely on devices such as Palm Pilots® and notebook computers to get you through the day is a direct measure of how willing you'd be to accept technology-based marine guidance systems. Depending on your view of computers, you might think of electronic charting as computerized navigation, propeller-head skippering, being lazy or just simply taking advantage of technology. Any way you cut it, getting from place to place on the water by means of computers is actually a rather straightforward concept that is anything but a lazy man's approach.

The Basics

Although the devices have changed over the years as a result of advances in satellite communications, finding your position on the surface of the earth has been possible for a long

Electronics Aboard -- By Stephen Fishman

time. As it relates to maritime positioning, we've had devices at our disposal for more than 25 years that could tell us where on the planet we were, with an error of no more than approximately 50 feet.

With the advent of the Global Positioning System (GPS) and its series of enhancements, we can now pinpoint our location with an error of less than 10 feet. Imagine, we can go anywhere in the world and know where we are within less than 3 meters!

The essence of electronic navigation is connecting a GPS to a computer running software on a hard drive or a CD-ROM that includes electronic versions of government paper charts. The software shows you, in monochrome or color, where you are on its chart display, where you're going, how fast you're going and how well you're following the course you planned to take.

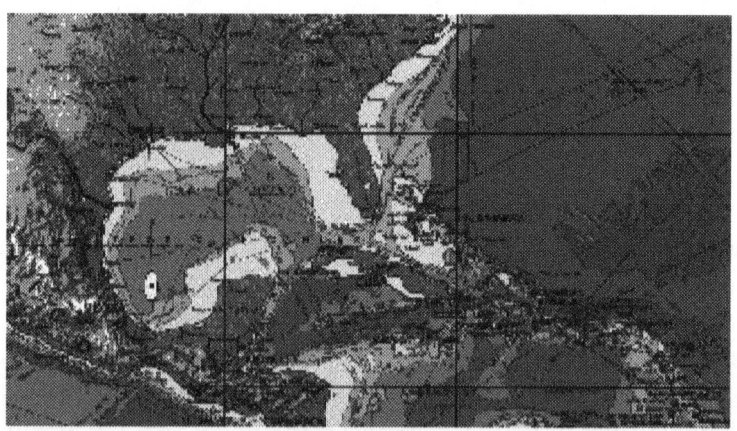

Figure 6-1

Typical small scale electronic chart (Maptech)

The display can also show you tides and currents in the area as well as channel markers, lighthouses, submerged dangers, the water depth, etc. The electronic chart can also calculate the bearing and distance from your boat to any other object on the chart and how long it will take you to get there at

Electronics Aboard -- By Stephen Fishman

your present speed. In fact, you can actually watch a representation of your vessel move across the chart, matching your real movement across the water and changing as your boat speed changes.

Fixed aspects of a typical display also include shipping lanes, harbor entrance paths and color interpretations of varying water depths.

One of the really nice things about electronic charting software is, when you reach the edge of one chart, the program is smart enough to know which chart is needed next. With little ado, it retrieves the correct chart from the hard drive and continues your passage across the screen.

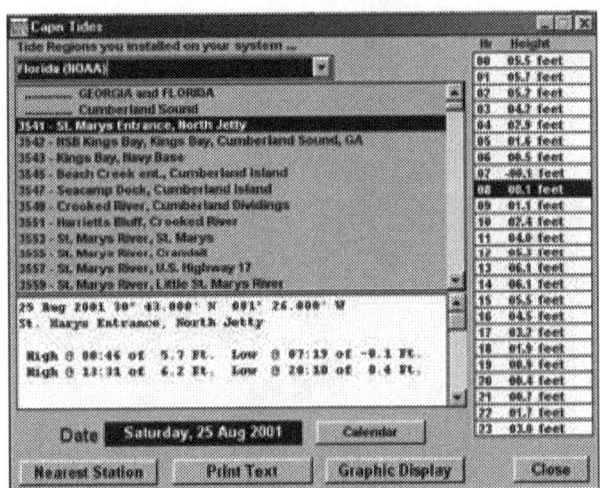

Figure 6-2

Sample Tide Table Display (The Cap'n)

To prevent cluttering up the display with potentially unwanted data, most of this information stays hidden beneath the surface of the chart until you want to know about something in particular.

A charting program is, fundamentally, a large database of information to which you can add all sorts of data. This can include waypoints on a route, a fishing spot, the location of a protected cove or even the location of your favorite waterside restaurant.

The database comes from the vendor with an incredible host of information already programmed into the software. A few items are U.S. government light lists, celestial navigation tables, tides and currents, state and country abbreviations, etc.

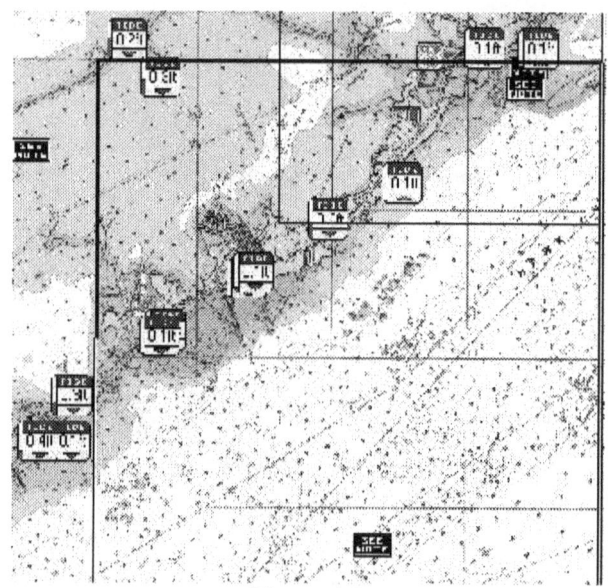

Figure 6-3

Graphical tides display. Block insets show tide information. (Maptech)

Coming & Going

A charting program can tell you not only where you are and where you've been, but it can also show you how to get where you want to go. Charting programs provide a visual, click-here approach to route planning that facilitates planning a journey down the river, along a coastline or across an ocean.

In fact, if charting programs do nothing else, they encourage detailed planning in a way that no other navigation

Electronics Aboard -- By Stephen Fishman

method or product can. Imagine, in the comfort of your cozy home you can plan your next seagoing adventure, even if it won't begin for months. You can plan each waypoint and every course change. You can familiarize yourself with typical tides in the area for the time of year you'll be traveling, as well as the particulars of local currents. You'll have the luxury of fully investigating - and committing to memory - where the shallows are located, where wrecks lurk just beneath the surface and the type of marker lights you will see.

If you're as prudent as most skippers planning an extended voyage, you'll make sure your mate knows some of the same data you do. In the event of an emergency or if the weather takes a turn for the worst, you have a backup plan immediately available because you've entered foreign waters armed with incredible amounts of local knowledge.

When all the planning and preparation is complete, you can save the details of your trip for later recall, printing or editing. Charting programs are limited only by the storage capacity of the hard drive and the imagination of the navigator.

Backups

I'm convinced it can't be said too often: Always have a navigation backup plan for your electronic charts. Electric devices can fail, batteries can become depleted unexpectedly and errant information can be inadvertently entered. At the very least, note two types of data into a log – hourly plots and every waypoint you pass along your route. If all of your electronics go down at the same time, you'll know your position from no more than an hour previously and that could make all the difference.

Whether your travels take you to foreign ports or just down the coast, paper charts can get you out of trouble and keep you out of trouble if the need arises. A set of paper charts isn't the cheapest purchase you'll ever make, but it's the best travel insurance you'll ever buy if you're planning on an open water passage.

Electronics Aboard -- By Stephen Fishman

Of course, this admonition is based on the assumption that you actually know how to use plotting tools such as parallel rules, dividers and a compass. If you don't, consider this: One of the best investments you can make is a course in paper charting and navigation. Two readily available sources of navigation training are the U.S. Power Squadron and, in some areas, the U.S Coast Guard Auxiliary. For a nominal fee (usually about $25), you can sign up for a six-week course that will teach you the mechanics of navigation. The course includes, how to plot a dead reckoning (DR) position on a chart and how to really use a compass.

Even if you never have to apply to a paper chart what you learn in class, the course will leave you with more confidence and an increased feeling of self-sufficiency.

Not Just A Fancy Map

To the uninitiated, electronic charts might appear to be nothing more than colorful maps presented in a convenient way, but nothing could be further from the truth. In short, maps show you what's on the dirt while charts show you what's on the water.

Electronic nautical charts are the alter ego of traditional terrestrial maps. The charts show very few land-based details, while offering incredible amounts of waterborne data. Typically, charts show only those details that impact a mariner, including lighthouses, docks, piers, and marinas, marine-related service businesses and coastal government offices concerned with maritime activities.

Electronic charting programs have become quite sophisticated and are expressly designed with the voyaging boater in mind, offering operating considerations such as these:

You always know where you are. Charting software shows your vessel's position either with a boat symbol or with crosshairs, and is one of only a handful of display parameters

Electronics Aboard -- By Stephen Fishman

for which there are no options. Along with the vessel's symbol, the latitude and longitude are also always displayed.

Notebook computer use. Keep in mind that portable computers are not as powerful as their desktop counterparts even if the specifications are identical. This is an important point relative to performance of the system. Still, contemporary notebook systems are far more powerful than their desktop cousins were only a few years ago.

Oversize electronic buttons and controls. When you're on a moving, pitching platform your aim is likely to be off a bit, and this consideration helps makes a mouse or touchpad more useful.

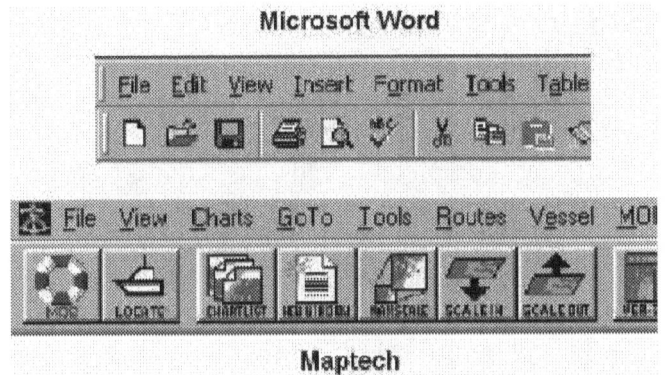

Figure 6-4

Toolbar comparison

Labels on buoys and waypoints. This eliminates the annoyance of having to display a light list in order to find out if a given buoy has a bell, or how often a light flashes and in what color. Position labels also simplify the task of knowing where you are along your course, instead of having to search a course leg to learn which waypoint is next.

Labels are transparent and in contrasting colors. This is a VERY big deal, given the potential profusion of labels in a channel or at the entrance to a harbor. Transparent labels let you see the information beneath, while a variety of

Electronics Aboard -- By Stephen Fishman

contrasting colors make buoys stand out from the chart and a clue about the type of marker.

Measurements units are user selectable. Most software programs offer you the option of choosing between nautical miles and statute miles, with nautical miles being the default. Depths can be displayed as feet, meters or fathoms with feet preset as the default for most programs.

In addition, measurements can be changed quickly as needed and, in some software, even automatically when it makes sense to do so. For example, *The Cap'n* charting program automatically shifts from nautical miles to yards for distances of less than half a mile, and with good reason. Can you imagine trying to deal with a distance of .057 nautical miles when 100 yards is so much more familiar?

Nighttime display. The rigors of standing watch after dark would be far more difficult without a way of maintaining your night vision. Although it's much easier to navigate with a color chart, a completely red display is an excellent compromise. Switching from a normal display to a night vision display preserves all of the chart's detail but shows it to you in shades of red.

Chart orientation. Just like paper charts, electronic charts can be rotated to a position that's most comfortable for you, and most charting programs offer three options:

• *North up*, which orients the chart to magnetic north
• *Heading up*, which orients the chart to your general course direction
• *Leg up*, which orients the top of the chart for the specific leg on which you're traveling. This view will change automatically when you turn to a new leg of your course, and can be disconcerting if adjoining legs have radically different relative bearings

Celestial navigation. Many programs include sight-reduction tables as well as an electronic version of an almanac. This means that celestial navigation data is built-in for sailors who know how to use it, and available with tutorials for people who want to learn.

This is by no means a complete list of design criteria. The current crop of charting products makes onboard navigation easier than it's ever been, especially for the novice mariner.

The Practical Side

Most navigation programs also have similarities in essential functions, ship's operations and information retrieval. Again, a complete list would require far more space than we have here, but some of the more significant common features are these:

- Chart display options that include overlays of tides, currents, markers and waypoints or nothing but the chart
- Preprogrammed waypoints and courses for popular routes and destinations
- The ability to upload and download waypoints from a wide variety of GPS units
- High resolution "zoom in" control that magnifies small areas of a chart while maintaining a wealth of detail
- A legal navigation log of each journey that is automatically created and maintained
- Tracking ship's inventory of supplies and spare parts along with maintenance schedules and records
- Easy, fast retrieval of extensive information on thousands of ports around the world
- Let's you print reduced size charts on letter and legal size paper, or print a chart full size on multiple pages of paper

As with charting functions, the list of general operations is a long one. It suffices to say that you're unlikely to be dissatisfied with any charting program.

Electronics Aboard -- *By Stephen Fishman*

Final Points

If you decide to invest in charting software, be aware that the computer you choose will either make or break you as an electronic navigator. Notebook computers are by far the most popular choice, but a high-end notebook PC can be expensive, especially in a configuration for charting.

At a minimum, I recommend nothing less than a 600MHz processor, 256MB of RAM and a color TFT LCD screen that is as large as your budget will allow or, even better, a large standalone LCD display.

Electronic charting is incredibly demanding on a computer's resources. It's unlikely that your notebook computer will ever be asked to handle anything so processor-intensive. The specifications above should be considered minimums, the more horsepower and memory, the better.

Electronics Aboard -- By Stephen Fishman

Chapter Seven
Chartplotters

A chartplotter offers perhaps the greatest potential for navigation capability of all the current electronic navigation aids. It combines electronic charts, dynamic memory and input capability with a high-resolution monochrome or color display to provide position information that is readily understood with little regard for the instruction manual. This last point alone could make the investment worthwhile.

By itself, a chartplotter is similar to an intelligent pet waiting for his master's command. However, once the chartplotter begins receiving position data from an outside source, such as a GPS, it can respond in many ways to assist you in accurately navigating your vessel.

You might think of a chartplotter as an independent service provider that can deliver a host of functions after it knows what you want to see and do. Among other things, a chartplotter can provide these major functions:

- Calculate the distance and bearing to any object on a chart
- Lay in a course with the bearing, range and position of each waypoint
- Track your boat's progress along a predetermined course and calculate the differential (error), if any
- Store multiple charts, often referred to as "chart packs", for a particular locale
- To the extent of its memory, store multiple courses for

Electronics Aboard -- By Stephen Fishman

future recall
- Enable alarms that alert you to charted hazards, off-course conditions or your arrival at a waypoint
- Steer the vessel from one waypoint to another

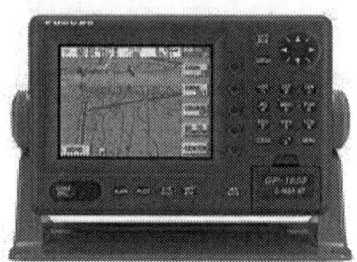

Figure 7-1

Typical chartplotter

The Basics & Then Some

A chartplotter can be a video chart to me, a fishfinder to you and a radar to someone else. It can be a stand-alone, jack-of-all-trades, providing any one of many displays depending upon the data stream from an input device. It can be a homogenous device blending information displays from two or more input devices simultaneously.

For example, a video plotter might display an electronic chart for waypoint-to-waypoint navigation based upon input from a GPS, or it might be a combination fishfinder and Loran. In either case, the capabilities far exceed simple chart display.

Even with all it can do, there are many skippers that wouldn't give a spliced eye for a chartplotter. They view it more as an interesting electronic gadget than as a serious navigation tool. This perspective may be valid to a point, but believing a chartplotter is no more than an electronic version of a set of paper charts is shortsighted. You may or may not agree with the following arguments, but they do give pause for thought.

Reliability of the device. True to a point, since 12-volt current is required. If the batteries die, so does the chartplotter. Paper charts should always be onboard.

High cost. Paper charts show at least as much detail as electronic charts – and sometimes more – and for a lot less money. This is a valid point in some instances but not all. Without exception, an electronic "chart pack" contains scores of charts for a region much like a chart book. If duplicated in single NOAA chart paper versions, the same electronic charts would cost the same or less.

The question is whether or not you would actually buy ALL of the NOAA charts for a particular region, and the answer is invariably "no." Chart-for-chart, paper charts are cheaper. But comparing an entire region of paper charts to an entire region of electronic charts is likely to reveal a chart pack as the bigger bargain of the two.

Difficult to read. This is true on the surface, since many LCD and video displays are simply not bright enough to be useful on deck or in the cockpit. But a fair comparison of practical use may reveal something else.

Almost without exception, paper charts are spread out for use on a large table inside the vessel. Even aboard the largest vessels, paper charts are only used in enclosed, weather-protected areas. This is a critical point because it negates the primary issue of readability difficulties in the cockpit.

With rare exception, chartplotters are also meant to be used in a protected area below decks and, in this environment, they are incredibly easy to view.

Encourages navigation mishaps. Supposedly, chartplotters are so easy to use that no one will bother with paper charts at all. The argument is especially oppressive regarding new sailors and the relatively little training needed to use an electronic chart versus a paper chart. Naysayers are quick to accuse skippers who rely upon electronic aids as being negligent in backing up electronic plots with paper plots and ignoring the basic tenet of making log entries.

Whether or not this is true depends on the individual

Electronics Aboard -- By Stephen Fishman

skipper and his, or her, view of risk-taking as it relates to life and limb.

It can be said, with at least some certainty, that skippers who rely totally on electronic charts are more likely to find themselves in trouble if problems occur. This is due to the fact that video charts can often carry less complete information than paper charts.

In all fairness to longtime navigators, there is nothing to compare with a complete set of paper charts for a specific region. Especially when it comes to ease of recovery from an errant plot and completeness of information for the region.

The caveat to remember is: "Don't rely on only one method."

Charts Are Charts, Right?

If you've ever used a paper chart, you know there's a lot of data as well as reference information. These include such things as scales along the sides of the chart, true north deviation, water depths, hazards to navigation, aids to navigation, coastlines, etc. Much of this information is color-coded with shallow water shown in blue and deep water shown in white, buoys marked in purple, channel lights colored in either red or green, and so forth. The legends, colors and symbols are consistent from one paper chart to the next, but this is not always true with electronic charts.

There are two types of electronic charts – raster and vector. Of the two, rasterized charts are preferred by most skippers because they look identical to their paper cousins, and are complete with the same color-coding, symbols, etc.

Raster charts are customarily supplied by vendors either in cartridges that plug in to the chartplotter or CD-ROMs intended for downloading to a hard drive. Unfortunately, there is no single standard within the marine industry for either the physical configuration of the cartridge or the data format of the charts. Cartridges aren't cheap, currently

Electronics Aboard -- By Stephen Fishman

costing about $300 each. Three formats – C-Map NT©, Navonics© and Garmin G-Charts© - are beginning to emerge as potential standards, but none have clearly taken the lead.

Vector charts don't look anything at all like their paper chart brethren. Vector charts are digitized from the originals, which means they are traced and data is added layer by layer until it contains as much information as the vendor wishes to provide. As a result, vector charts don't contain as much data as raster charts and are generally intended for monochrome display.

Vector charts typically show the shoreline, some navigation aids and depth curves, but not depth numbers. Commonly missing from vector charts are symbols for submerged objects, underwater cables, rocks and actual depth soundings. This essentially makes them simplified versions of the original paper charts from which they were drawn. But vector charts have some redeeming values that make them quite attractive in spite of their shortcomings.

Perhaps most important, vector charts require only a fraction of the processor horsepower and dynamic memory that raster charts require. This allows you to store more charts in any given media, and they can be handled by the computer far more quickly as you reach the edge of one chart and another is needed for display. Smaller storage requirements also mean you'll get more for your money when you buy cartridges or CDs of electronic charts. For instance, it's fairly common for a C-Map cartridge to contain as many as 75 vector charts in the rough equivalent of about 1MB of storage, while an entire CD-ROM with 650MB of storage may be needed for the same number of raster charts.

One of the great things about a vector chart, is the displayed symbols and other data can be selectively removed. As mentioned previously, vector charts are digitized in layers much like making a sandwich consisting of various layers of ingredients. These layers can be selectively removed to simplify the chart display or added to increase its usefulness. A hard copy can be easily made of the modified chart display so you'll

Electronics Aboard -- By Stephen Fishman

have a backup in case of a power failure or for record-keeping and log entries.

Both types of charts can be updated but raster charts are typically updated only after the government has revised the official originals. Vector charts can be updated by the vendor since these are digitized, hand-drawn reproductions of the originals.

No doubt, raster charts will eventually provide the ability to selectively remove data displayed on the chart but, for now at least, this remains one of the greatest strengths of vector charts. The other primary advantage of vector charts is a significantly reduced need for high-end processing capacity. This translates into less expensive products since the charts are graphically simpler.

Even given this reduced complexity, raster charts offer unmatched accuracy and faithfulness to the original.

Chart Utopia

One last thing before we leave the topic of the charts themselves. There has been an initiative for years to standardize cartography worldwide. The intent is providing all charts on a 1:1 scale in computer memory so they can be rescaled by the user as needed. The idea is to eliminate the somewhat confusing array of overlapping paper charts and charts of varying scales – large-scale and small-scale charts, as they are called.

If this international hydrographic heaven were to be realized, you would select the area, or areas, of the world's waterways you want to see and order them in one of two ways, or both:

- In electronic form to suit your navigation system, and then download it to your computer
- Buy the charts in paper form from a marine supplier who, in turn, orders the charts from a printer linked to a global cartography database

Electronics Aboard -- By Stephen Fishman

Although this scenario might seem a bit farfetched right now, there is a lot of evidence that it may actually become a reality in the foreseeable future.

Choices & Control

If you venture even a short distance from land or you're prone to revisit the same weekend destinations, there is probably a chartplotter with your name on it.

Figure 7-2

Chartplotter display

It could be a simple monochrome display that comes to life only when it receives data from an external GPS. It could be a sophisticated unit with its own built-in differential GPS and a color display.

Figure 7-3

Integrated DGPS chartplotter

Electronics Aboard -- By Stephen Fishman

Chartplotters typically have these controls:

Trackpad: Similar to a trackball attached a computer. It moves the cursor in any direction and the progress can be seen on the display. Although weather and water-resistant, a trackpad and the balance of the controls on most chartplotters are not waterproof.

Cursor: Displayed as a moving cross-hair, often with arrows on the ends, indicating compass directions. On most chartplotters, the cursor is context-sensitive, which means that it will pop up different information depending upon where it's placed.

For example, many chartplotters display position data when the cursor is placed over a lighthouse or other item in a major light list. Some units also display detailed information on a status bar - at the top or bottom of the screen - in a manner similar to the way information looks in a Microsoft® Windows® application.

Some chartplotters pop up sub-menus of options when the cursor is placed over an object such as a waypoint. Most models change the function of the cursor from a floating pointer to a menu selector when additional menus are displayed.

Dedicated keys: Specific function keys that simplify the operation of the chartplotter. Examples of dedicated keys are functions such as GoTo, Range, Clear and Enter keys. Often, each key has a dual mode that provides one function when pressed and released, and another when pressed and held down.

Soft keys: Multifunction keys that can be programmed to perform a variety of functions. Although found only on the higher-end models, soft keys typically have context-sensitive functions that change with the mode of operation, display or position of the cursor.

For example, a soft key might perform as many as three functions:

Electronics Aboard -- By Stephen Fishman

- Waypoint insertion when a coastal chart is on the screen alone
- A vessel marker when a radar display is overlayed on top of a chart
- A function selector when sub-menus appear

Status bar: Displays data relative to the current operation.

Function bar: This bar may be present in addition to a status bar. Almost without exception, if a function bar is present it's displayed on the opposite side of the screen from the status bar to minimized confusion.

A function bar differs from a status bar. A function bar generally provides access to more options shows a list of sub-menus, a light list or other data source, or be a route to additional menus.

Pop-up menus: The route through virtually all of the options provided by a chartplotter. Although some functions can be directly accessed by means of dedicated keys, pop-up menus and their associated sub-menus lead you through the myriad of possible ways in which the unit can be used.

All of the information used by the chartplotter, as well as all of the course data you enter, is stored in the unit's memory in the form of databases. When a database such as a light list is displayed, you can select an item from the list and add it to the chart, find out more about it, or eliminate it from the chart. This is dependent upon the type of chart (vector or raster) and the mode in which the chartplotter is being used.

Electronics Aboard -- By Stephen Fishman

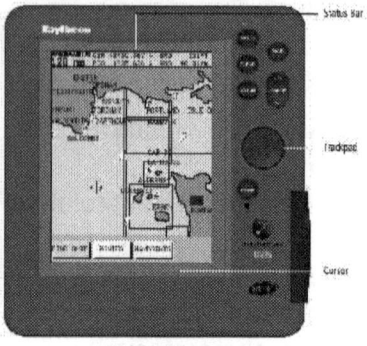

Figure 7-4

Raytheon model 425 chartplotter

Too Much Information

When IBM first introduced the personal computer over two decades ago, one of the biggest complaints about the product was that it was too complicated to use. This was certainly true. What exacerbated the problem was the fact that there was so much that could be done with this new device, and there were so many choices of software to do it. All but the most die-hard of electronics geeks and serious business users turned away from the technology.

For many years, this was the general attitude towards chartplotters, too. During the past few years especially, chartplotters have grown in complexity as a result of offering more features and combinations of functionality. The range of currently available products spans the spectrum from a "drone" unit requiring input to be even marginally useful, to a top-of-the-line integrated system with a chartplotter, depth sounder, GPS and DGPS.

Fortunately, most chartplotters now offer a simulation mode that, like a tutorial for a personal computer program, leads you through function, capabilities and purpose. Even a cursory glance at a screen display reveals there is much to know and learn before putting a chartplotter through its paces.

Caution! *Never use simulated data or sample course plots for actual navigation.*

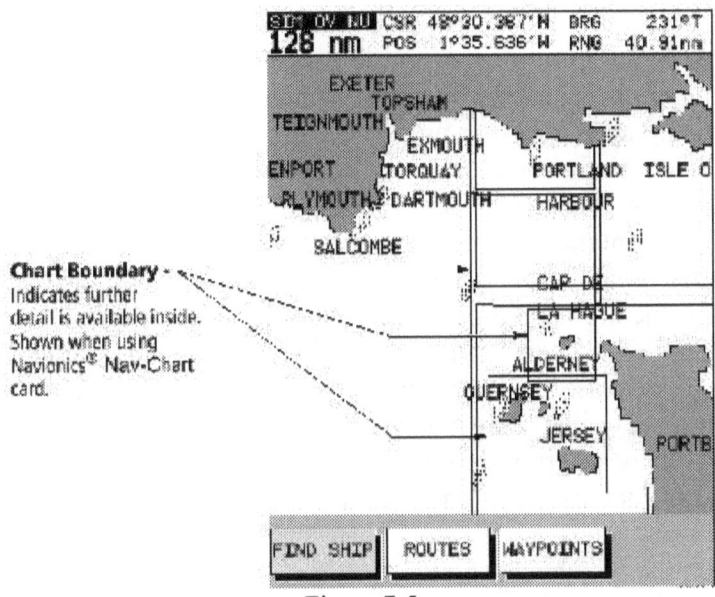

Figure 7-5

Typical screen display and chart outlines

Truly User Friendly

You don't need to know computers, you don't even need to draw a straight line. There is no "code" to type or cryptic messages to decipher. In fact, creating a course – a route comprised of several legs – is one of the easiest of all tasks to accomplish.

To create a course with most chartplotters, simply place the cursor on a starting point and press the ENTER key. Then move the cursor to the next waypoint – a turn along the way or perhaps a destination – and press ENTER again. A line will automatically be drawn between the two positions. The

Electronics Aboard -- *By Stephen Fishman*

good news is that this can be done either while underway or while you're still in the slip. But wait, that's not all. If you have accidentally drawn the leg of a course that's too close to a shoreline, or other obstruction, most chartplotters let you to select the leg and drag it away from the danger. The unit will then automatically redraw the single leg as two legs while circumventing the danger in the process. When you've plotted a course, the data can be saved to memory and the course can be redisplayed at a later time.

The chartplotter can also display a course as a list of waypoints that make log entries a breeze. Thanks to the plotter's memory, you can create an entire voyage before leaving your home port, including fuel stops, sightseeing, bridge locations, and other important navigation data. Further, virtually all plotters have a "zoom" feature. This feature allows you to increase the magnification of a selected area of a chart from a view that shows an entire ocean, to another view that shows only a harbor entrance. Details such as lights, buoys and hazards increase in number as the magnification of the chart increases, and the plotter automatically changes scales to match the area being shown.

Most units also have a dedicated key that displays position information for your boat, as well as the lat/lon of all waypoints visible on the screen. To make this data even more meaningful, the display typically shows your actual course along with the plotted course. This gives you a quick and easy method of recognizing the effects of wind and currents on your progress.

Depending on the make and model, a chartplotter might have enough memory to store 100 waypoints or several thousand. You can choose to hold your vessel in the center of the display while the chart "moves" under it or you can show your boat moving across the chart in the actual direction of travel.

Since a chartplotter is based on computer technology, you have a host of calculation functions at your disposal. These include such things as fuel consumption, estimated time of arrival, estimated number of hours left until you reach your destination, the distance you've traveled, the number of appointments you've missed. Well, maybe not the appointments, but who cares?

What's The Catch?

The catch is the same as always when it comes to marine electronics of any type – power consumption and cost. The more capable the unit, the more it will cost and the more DC power it will draw from the ship's batteries. But this is an oversimplification.

Cost is directly related to features and functionality. Vendor reputation aside, units with similar features are priced about the same regardless of the manufacturer. The greatest difference in the price of one unit over another is found in the degree the unit integrates various functions. Does the plotter combine a GPS/DGPS and a depth sounder together? Is it a combination GPS and radar system in a chartplotter package? Or maybe the plotter melds a Loran system with a fishfinder.

One of the best things about this integration is the price of multifunction chartplotters is usually less than the total price of individual components. If you think about it, it makes sense. One product that includes a chartplotter, GPS and fishfinder eliminates a lot of costs – one enclosure instead of three, electronic components that share functions, a single mounting system, a single shipping carton, perhaps fewer transducers, etc.

All of these combinations provide enhanced convenience, reduced space requirements at the helm and lower costs than buying the various components as separate units. But what happens if the GPS section dies? Is the entire chartplotter useless? Will the radar component still function if the fishfinder portion gets confused? Is the cost of repair greater than if these systems were segregated? It all depends on the system you chose so the most current information will be obtained from your local dealer .

Electronics Aboard -- By *Stephen Fishman*

Then there's the issue of power. If you've installed individual units for chart plotting, locating fish and navigating by radar, for instance, you can select which devices to use and which to turn off. This reduces power consumption which, on a sailboat, can be a critical issue. Even aboard a powerboat, do you really want to run everything all of the time? Chartplotters that combine other functions, such as a GPS, typically have a higher electrical demand than these same devices would have individually. At the same time, it can be argued that an integrated system uses less power than its total individual components would use if they were all turned on and operating.

Alarms

Alarms are often overlooked when discussing the features of a chartplotter. They can alert you to dangers such as headlands, platforms and rigs. With the help of a depth sounder, they will get your attention if a submerged object intercepts your course.

They can also remind you where to turn as you approach a waypoint. For example, if you've selected a buoy as a turning point, an alarm can sound as your approach takes you within a predetermined minimum distance of the mark. One caution, though. Even the most accurate of navigation systems will be off by a few feet, so be sure to leave yourself a margin of error to avoid hitting the mark before the alarm tells you that you've arrived at the waypoint.

An alarm can also keep you abreast of variances from your course. Most chartplotters have the ability to set lines on the screen that parallel your course, providing a limit for how much course variance can occur before an alarm will sound.

Many systems have an alarm that can be used when a radar display overlays the course display. This type of alarm duplicates the function of a radar proximity alarm that sounds when objects, such as other boats, approach to within a predetermined minimum distance. Invariably, this type of alarm

Electronics Aboard -- By Stephen Fishman

works in conjunction with a course display.

With all this technology available at your finger tips it is easy to understand why chartplotters become more popular with each passing year.

Electronics Aboard -- *By Stephen Fishman*

Electronics Aboard -- By Stephen Fishman

Chapter Eight
Autopilots

Of all the equipment you will install on your boat, I can think of nothing that will bring more pleasure over a longer period of time and a wider range of activities than an autopilot. Interestingly, an autopilot is nearly always one of the last gadgets a boater will buy.

Invented by Elmer Sperry, autopilots can be a blessing or a curse, depending upon who you talk to and when they bought their unit. If it was a decade ago, chances are they paid a king's ransom for the system and got little more than aggravation in return. On the other hand, today's autopilots can repay their cost many times over in convenience and relaxation.

Autopilots are, arguably, the single most complicated subsystem on board, with the notable exception of the running gear, due to their combination of electrical and mechanical components as well as electronics.

My Story

For many years, my wife and I lived aboard a 32-foot sailboat. She (the boat) was big for a 32-footer, but she was still only 32 feet long. As liveaboards, our priorities regarding electronics tended to be more closely aligned with what you might expect to find in a house than what you might find on a boat – television and stereo first, and boating stuff second. Once the "essential" creature comforts had been addressed, we

Electronics Aboard -- By Stephen Fishman

turned our attention to marine navigation in preparation for many anticipated offshore vacation voyages.

We already had a VHF radio, of course, but beyond that there was little else on board that would have been of much value in a seaway. Like most other boaters, we perused the cataloges and showrooms of marine suppliers in an effort to identify exactly what we needed – radar, GPS, etc - and what we were willing to pay to get. As luck would have it, we met an opinionated old salt one night in a dingy coastal tavern and were treated to a first-class tongue-lashing regarding our misplaced priorities.

In short, he told us we were full of it.

He was diplomatic and kind, asking gentle prodding questions like, "What do you wanna do…*steer* all the way to the Keys?" "Don't you two want to spend any time awake… *together*?" His laid-back style and beat-around-the-bush approach ultimately helped us see the error of our ways, and made one point crystal clear: The more automated the vessel, the more time you will have to enjoy the journey.

A Short Testimonial

I think it's important for you to know that I don't like steering. The boating cliché of the man behind the wheel, while the woman lounges on the foredeck or plays galley slave was never the family picture aboard *Lady Greyhawke*. I encouraged my wife to steer; in fact, I encouraged almost *any*one to steer so I wouldn't have to. Raise and trim sails, wrestle a whisker pole, set ground tackle, scrub the waterline. I would rather do anything – *anything* - than steer.

Now don't let anyone pull your halyard. Just because we lived aboard didn't mean we could leave the slip anytime we wanted. The same constraints that hold everyone else ashore held us – work, family, errands, etc. When we did slip our docklines, I did my level best to stay out from behind the wheel. Fortunately, this worked out well because Deborah, my wife, actually *liked* steering the boat.

Electronics Aboard -- By Stephen Fishman

Don't ask me why.

More than anything, an autopilot represents freedom. Freedom to set a course and relax as the boat steers herself. Freedom to chat with your significant other and not split your attention between your mate and steering. Autopilots take over the drudgery of steering so we can grab a cool drink from the fridge, use the head, make a sandwich or just relax in the cockpit. Steering a boat well is critical to efficiently reaching a destination along a predetermined course. It's also a mindless activity an autopilot can do better than a human, especially when steering continues hour after hour, 24-hours day for several days in a row. It may not be a big deal during a daysail on a familiar bay, but in the middle of the night when you're on watch alone, an autopilot can make all the difference.

If you're among those of us who sail alone as often as not, an autopilot can mean the difference between a relaxing evening sail after work or several more hours of working. For singlehanders on the open sea, an autopilot allows naps throughout the day, making nighttime watches safer for all concerned.

Another advantage of an autopilot that cannot be stressed enough is how much assistance it can provide in case of an emergency. Whether underway alone or with crew, an autopilot can allow everyone aboard to focus on solving a problem. The more experienced hands in any circumstance, the better.

An Autopilot Is

Essentially, an autopilot steers your boat on a heading you have entered into the control head manually or a heading provided by connecting a GPS or Loran to the pilot. When engaged, the pilot will do its best to maintain that course.

An autopilot is actually a combination of three components, including an electronic compass, the steering hardware, and an electronic control module. These components are different in their particulars for powerboats

Electronics Aboard -- By Stephen Fishman

and sailing craft, but their functions and general installation are the same.

The Compass

An electronic compass – a fluxgate compass, to be exact – has no readable display. It is mounted as near the centerline of the vessel as possible and as close to the waterline as practical. Although it's important to mount the compass in a dry area that's low in the boat, it's even more critical to make sure the compass is as far away as possible from all ferrous metals. This point can't be stressed enough because even something innocuous can cause a problem. In one sailboat, a vinyl-coated wire shelf contained enough metal – even with the plastic coating - to cause an error of nearly twenty degrees!

A fluxgate compass is more accurately termed a "heading sensor" since it has no display. Instead, it provides heading data for the control module which is translated into instructions for the pilot. The heading is displayed on the control module in an LCD window of three digits indicating a compass direction. Once calibrated, the heading display on the control module can easily be used as an alternative steering compass.

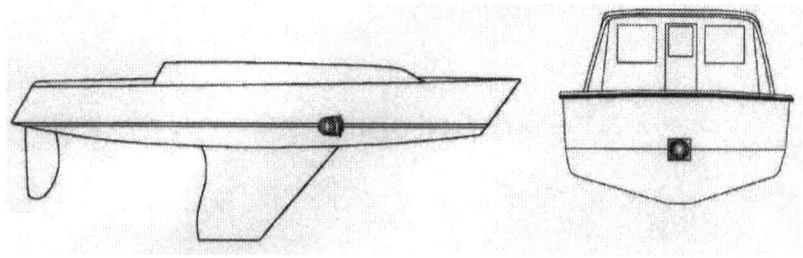

Figure 8-1

Electronic compass locations

To help ensure accuracy while underway, most fluxgates are gimbaled inside their housings so they can pivot

Electronics Aboard -- *By Stephen Fishman*

in at least two directions, a function of particular importance to sailboat skippers. The signal from the heading sensor updates the control module about four times a second. The control module compares the data to the actual course only about once every five seconds or so. This setting, found on most autopilots, directs the autopilot to make course adjustments more often or less often depending on the boat and sea conditions.

An alternative to steering with data from a fluxgate compass is steering by wind direction. Used almost exclusively on sailboats, many autopilots can be connected to a wind direction indicator in the cockpit that receives data from a masthead-mounted windvane. In practice, the autopilot is set to maintain a course relative to the wind direction as opposed to using a specific heading as a reference. This works well as long as the wind direction is constant, but if it changes and the autopilot isn't reset, you might end up a long way from where you wanted to be. If you're out for a daysail, this might be the preferred method of using an autopilot.

Connected to a control module by means of an electrical cable, the electronic compass constantly transmits directional data, in degrees. The compass is heavily damped to minimize the effects of yaw and pitch on the accuracy of the information sent to the control module. The compass does its job best when these effects are first minimized to the extent possible by its location on the boat.

For wheel steered boats, there are two basic types of autopilot systems – wheel pilots and below-deck pilots. To help you decide which autopilot might be best for your vessel, consider these four questions:

• What type of boat do you have - planing or displacement? A displacement vessel will require a more robust system than a planing vessel.
• What is the length and displacement of your vessel? Larger boats demand stronger systems, and most of these are below-deck models.

Electronics Aboard -- By Stephen Fishman

• Is the steering system mechanical or hydraulic? Most wheel pilots are designed for mechanical steering systems.
• Is your primary use of the boat in coastal or offshore waters? Bigger seas and stronger winds are good reasons to consider a below-deck autopilot.

The above-deck type – commonly called a wheel pilot is characterized by a plastic ring attached to the steering wheel.

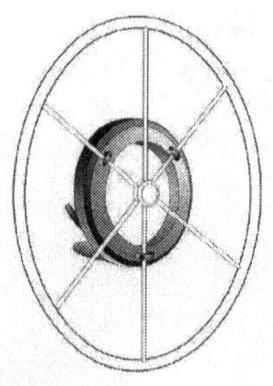

Figure 8-2

Wheel pilot

These rings are larger on sailboat steering wheels, of course, but they are both similar in that they mechanically attach to the spokes of an all metal steering wheel. The ring, in turn, connects to a gear or belt drive motor mounted on the pedestal. The drive mechanism is electrically connected to the control module by a cable. The entire system gets its power from the vessel's 12-volt, DC battery banks.

The drive mechanism rotates the steering wheel until the electronic compass tells the control module that the selected course has been achieved. In practical terms, this means that an autopilot will turn the boat from port to starboard in order to maintain whatever heading you have told the autopilot to steer.

Wheel pilots are generally the best choice for boats under 40 feet, and with a displacement of less than 20,000 pounds. This includes sailboats as well as most cabin cruisers, convertibles and cockpit motoryachts. Sportfishermen, performance boats and express cruisers up to 45 feet may be able to use a wheel pilot as a result of designs that reduce the weight of the vessel or keels that make them more directionally stable.

Below-deck autopilots also use a fluxgate compass located low in the boat as well as a control module in the cockpit or helm station, but the actual driving/steering mechanism is hidden away near the rudder.

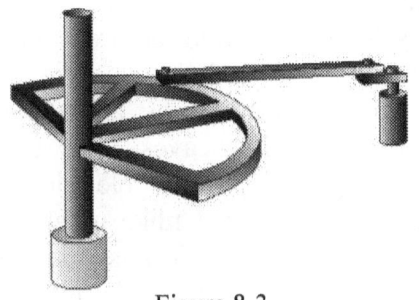

Figure 8-3

Below-deck pilot

Most below-deck pilots are mechanical in nature, with an actuating arm attached to the steering quadrant, and a drive motor attached to the arm. After a course has been entered and the autopilot has been engaged, the drive motor and actuating arm work to steer the boat from port to starboard in an effort to maintain the heading that the compass "sees." The steering wheel rotates as the drive mechanism steers the boat, but there is no sound of gears meshing. I've often felt it a little eerie to see a steering wheel turn on any boat – power or sail – without a sound.

A below-deck pilot can be far more expensive than a wheel pilot, but it's also more accurate and can handle heavy loads. Below-deck pilots are generally installed on boats 40 feet and longer since these vessels tend to have greater displacements that demand more robust steering components.

Powerboats Only

Another type of below-deck pilot, made almost exclusively for power vessels, is hydraulic and designed to interconnect parallel steering locations. Instead of an electric motor driving a mechanical arm linked to a rudder, these systems use the same principle as the braking systems in our automobiles. An actuating arm inside a sealed sleeve moves the rudder when fluid inside the tubing is pressurized.

These systems are often favored for vessels with a flybridge, tuna tower or other elevated steering station. Hydraulic lines can be hidden almost anywhere, they eliminate the need for cables and sheaves, and they simplify the installation by letting you put the electric pump and other components almost anywhere. Unlike mechanical below-deck units, a hydraulic system duplicates the existing steering network of cables and can act as a backup if needed.

The single greatest disadvantage of a hydraulic system is an increased drain on the ship's batteries. This is overcome to a great extent because a powerboat engine runs constantly.

The Brain

No matter which system you install, you will always have a control unit in the cockpit or at the helm station. The control module is used to calibrate the system, and enter course and waypoint data.

Electronics Aboard -- By *Stephen Fishman*

Figure 8-4

Autopilot control module

The control module is invariably designed for permanent mounting somewhere near the steering wheel. Wired remote control units are available for many brands of autopilots, permitting as much as twenty-five feet of movement away from the helm. A wired remote will not usually offer all the controls of the primary control module, but you are typically able to make course changes in both fine (1 degree) and coarse (10 degree) increments.

Features common to most autopilot control modules, whether for power or sail, include:

- A backlit readout
- A combined numeric and graphical display
- Built-in SeaTalk, NMEA0183 or Ethernet protocol for integration with other devices
- Weather resistance
- 12-volt low battery drain (house banks)
- Multiple levels of rudder gain
- Adjustable turn rate of 5 degrees to 20 degrees
- Adjustable off-course alarm of 15 degrees to 40 degrees
- Red lighting for night use
- Data input from all other instruments and integration into a complete navigation system
- A connection to a GPS or Loran-C

Electronics Aboard -- *By Stephen Fishman*

For sailboat autopilots, additional features can include adjustable, automatic tacking and course control by means of wind direction.

A Few Details

Although the particulars of calibration and setup are different from one manufacturer to another, the general process is the same:

- Calibrate the compass
- Enter the compass deviation number into the control module
- Match the display on the control module to the ship's magnetic compass, assuming the vessel's steering compass has been "boxed" (calibrated, also called swinging the compass)
- Select operating parameters such as sensitivity and rudder control
- Store the configuration information

An autopilot is an extremely sophisticated piece of equipment. Even so, it's a stupid piece of gear until you tell it what it needs to know to do its job. For example, the pilot has no idea whether or not there is a cross-current, heavy winds or breaking seas. These all have a direct - and detrimental - effect on pilot performance and steering accuracy. For these reasons and others, almost all autopilot control modules require you to tell them what they need to know.

Sometimes called "sea state," this is a setting that represents the pilot's expected response to off-course steering corrections. All pilots work on the assumption that some tracking error is okay, but it's up to you to decide how much error should be allowed for your boat and its characteristics while underway. It doesn't take much imagination to appreciate the fact that a heavy displacement sailboat will react in a completely different way to sea conditions than a motoryacht of the same size.

What you're actually doing is setting the frequency of

Electronics Aboard -- By Stephen Fishman

course corrections. The less often the correction, the larger the error is likely to be, and vice versa. The catch here is that each correction requires electrical energy which, in turn, means that your batteries will drain faster if the pilot is working harder to maintain a course.

Sensitivity can be managed and its effect minimized by matching the amount of sail to the weather and waves, and properly trimming the sails. Aboard a powerboat, sensitivity issues can be minimized by reducing windage to the extent possible. This means stowing fenders, and removing or folding away unused biminis and awnings.

Gain

Also called rudder control, gain tells the autopilot how much rudder movement is required to make course corrections. Once again, the characteristics of the vessel come into play. Gain is often set in conjunction with a correction called "speed", a control that addresses the issue of how fast the correction is made. For example, a sailboat with a full-length keel needs more gain – more rudder effort – than an express cruiser with a planing hull, to make the same course change. At the same time, an express cruiser travels much faster than a sailboat so it needs a higher speed setting to make course corrections more quickly. If it weren't for this adjustable control, a high-speed boat might cover a substantial distance before adequate heading changes could be made.

Counter Rudder

This function is closely tied to the rudder speed setting just discussed. Regardless of the setting, a pilot can often overshoot the needed correction. This will cause the boat to wander back and forth along its course, never really settling into a "groove." Counter rudder works in much the same way as what we do when we're manual steering. To make a turn or change course, we turn the steering wheel in the direction we want to go but, if left in that position, we'll keep going in that direction and end up much further than we wanted. To keep that from happening, we turn the wheel back in the opposite direction before we get to our new heading. The counter rudder setting limits the amount of error the pilot is allowed to make when making course corrections.

Trim

This adjustment compensates for any ongoing sea condition that might affect the performance of the pilot. Examples of continuous circumstances might include a two-engine boat traveling with only one motor in operation, a heavy weather helm or perhaps a strong wind blowing in from one side of the boat. Basically what you're doing is telling the pilot that an off-center rudder position is temporarily equal to a rudder position that is straight on the centerline.

This is not a panacea for all sea conditions, since this setting will have no effect on drift that might result from a strong cross-wind. To correct this problem, a GPS or other position-finding device must be electronically incorporated into the system, and can calculate the amount of cross-track error. If a GPS is not in the system you'll have to input adjustments to your course manually at periodic intervals.

Either way, an autopilot can completely automate the complex task of steering or, at a minimum, make it more manageable when seas and weather pipe up.

An Automated Day

It's a perfect summer Saturday morning. The sky is a brilliant blue, puffy fair-weather clouds decorate the horizon, the temperature is moderate, the humidity is down and there is a ten-knot breeze out of the favored direction for your area. In short, it's a perfect weekend day. So, what do you do? Why

Electronics Aboard -- By Stephen Fishman

you do what anyone in their right mind would do on a day like this – you fill a cooler with lunch, snacks and drinks and head for the marina.

You arrive at the dock, transfer the goodies to your pride and joy, and slip your moorings as quickly as possible. You motor leisurely down the fairway, out through the marina entrance and follow the channel to the nearest open water. If you're like me, you can't wait to engage the autopilot at the first possible moment so you can sit back and relax, and enjoy a lazy day on the water.

Only one thing, you forgot one tiny, teeny detail. You forgot to tell your mechanical pilot where you want to go. Before you can give over the steering to the autopilot, you have to enter the heading you want to maintain. For ease, let's say that the heading is 090 degrees, which is due east. Enter this number in the control unit by steering your boat to that heading while watching the autopilot's LCD. When it shows 090, hold the course steady for several seconds and then engage the autopilot by flipping a lever or releasing a clamp, depending on the make and model of the pilot.

Alternatively, you can simply enter the heading you would like to take. In this instance, simply enter the numbers "090" on the autopilot control head, engage the pilot and you're done.

That's all there is to it; you are now free to move about the cabin. On a relatively calm day, you won't have to touch the system again until it's time to change course. Some models of sailboat autopilots will help a sailboat tack from port to starboard, or vice versa, by turning the boat 70 degrees or so to a new tack on the same heading while you reset the sails. For singlehand sailors, this is one of the most useful features an autopilot can provide, and an excellent reason for choosing one model over another.

As I said at the beginning of the chapter, an autopilot can cut the shackles that bind you to the steering wheel and let you fully enjoy your time afloat. Fair winds!

Electronics Aboard -- By Stephen Fishman

Electronics Aboard -- By *Stephen Fishman*

Chapter Nine
Radar

In times past, radar was an expensive and bulky navigation tool found on only the largest private yachts and military vessels. Things are a lot different today. Radar has become so compact even the smallest vessel has space to install a unit and is so reasonably priced, it fits the budget of almost any skipper. Equally important, is the ability of most radar sets to interconnect with other navigation instruments.

The word radar is an acronym meaning **RA**dio **D**etection **A**nd **R**anging. Radar works on the simple principle of reflection of microwaves. A radar measures the time it takes for a signal to reflect back from any object the signal can reach. Since some targets reflect back more of the original signal than other targets, some objects on a radar display appear brighter or larger than other objects of a similar size.

A radar alternately transmits and receives pulses of microwave wavelengths from 1 centimeter to 1 meter in size. The corresponding frequency range is 300MHz (megahertz) to 30GHz (gigahertz). In addition, a radar also sends and receives polarizations, which are waves that have been polarized in either a single vertical or single horizontal plane.

Radar pulses travel at the speed of light, giving new meaning to the term real-time calculations. The interval between the time a pulse is transmitted and the time it's echo is received is almost instantaneous. This incredibly small measure of time is divided in half to determine the distance of an object from the antenna. Since calculations are based upon such a short time span, radar has the ability to constantly update the position and distance of objects with virtually no delay relative to the location of the radar.

An Example

An easy way to understand this concept is to imagine standing on the edge of the Grand Canyon and shouting across the enormous gap beneath you. Your voice will eventually reach the cliffs on the opposite side of the canyon and bounce back to you. If you could measure the time delay between the shout and when you heard your echo, you could divide the time in half to determine a one-way amount of time. Multiply this time by the speed of sound, which is about 1,100 feet per second, and you have the distance between you and the cliff on the opposite side.

Functionally, radar performs two primary calculations – distance and relative bearing from the source. It then displays objects on a high-resolution display. After the distance to the object and its bearing are known, we can make decisions as to how close we want to be to these objects and, if necessary, how best to steer around them.

But radar is a lot smarter than just showing us what's there. Modern radar systems, even for recreational craft, can display this visual information in color and interface with other navigation devices such as a GPS. In general, it can make our lives much less complicated and safer in all types of weather conditions.

No Blind Eye

Unlike navigation aids such as buoys, channel markers, flashing lights and horns, radar works as well in dense fog as it does in brilliant sunshine. A radar can always "see," whether we can or not, which is why radar is so popular among skippers who are on the water in all sorts of weather, by

Electronics Aboard -- By Stephen Fishman

accident or by design.

Radar depends upon flat surfaces on the target for signal reflection to work, which is why metal ships and buildings on shore show up so clearly on a radar screen. Other objects such as buoys, for example, that are cylindrical in shape make poor reflectors, but those topped with crossed flat plates are easily seen and displayed.

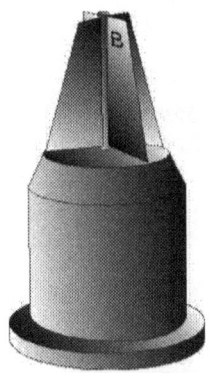

Figure 9-1

Harbor buoy

A radar reflector hoisted high in the rigging of a fiberglass sailboat can result in a high-visibility image on a radar display. This occurs even though little else aboard is capable of significant reflection.

The Antenna

A radar antenna is actually a transceiver, which means that it both transmits a signal and receives one. As with other antennas, it works best and has the longest range when mounted as high as possible on the vessel. Unlike static antennas for other devices, such as marine VHF radio, a radar antenna broadcasts its signal in all directions by rotating an aerial called a scanner. The longer the aerial, the narrower and more focused the transmitted beam of microwave energy. A narrower beam is desirable because it can produce more accurate distance and bearing calculations, as well as sharper displayed images.

There are two types of radar antennas – open array and closed array. The open array is characterized by an exposed rotating aerial sitting atop a bulbous base. A closed array antenna is usually referred to as a radome due to its dome-shaped housing. As you might expect, both types have advantages and disadvantages for pleasure boats.

The open array system consists of a rectangular bar (scanner), ranging in length from three feet to nine feet, rotating in a clockwise direction that feeds data to a transceiver mounted inside its base. Information is sent to the display unit in the cabin or to a steering station by means of a coaxial cable.

Figure 9-2

Open array antenna

Figure 9-3

Radome antenna

A closed array antenna also has a rotating scanner, but the aerial is enclosed inside the same housing as the transceiver. Most radomes are either 20-inches in diameter or 36-inches in diameter, but the scanner inside has to be smaller than this exterior dimension. As a result, most radome scanners are typically either 15-inches or 30-inches, respectively.

Radomes find a home most commonly on sailboats and fishing boats where lines and rigging might foul the rotating bar of an open array. This is not to say that open arrays are not found on sailboats; quite the contrary, but the boats must be larger or have special provisions such as guards or extended mounts to protect the array.

Open array radars have a longer range due to their longer aerials, and produce a narrower beam than a closed array system of the same size.

Before continuing, a few definitions are in order.

Transmission power. Stated in kilowatts (kW), this is a measure of the radar's ability to send a strong signal which, in turn, produces a strong echo. Transmission power is not usually a critical issue when buying a radar since most skippers tend to use a 4-mile range setting almost all the time.

Maximum range. The stated maximum distance that the transceiver can produce useful images on a display. This is usually stated in terms of transmitting power and miles of coverage. For example, a typical radome might have a power rating of 2.2kW (kilowatts) and a range of 24 nautical miles, while an open array unit might carry a power rating of 4kW and a range of 36 nautical miles.

Most recreational boaters, however, are not able to take advantage of a radar's maximum range because, in most cases, the array can't be mounted high enough off the water to achieve the optimum. Obviously, a sailboat will come closer to using the maximum potential range of a radar than will a power vessel of a similar size.

Minimum range. This is the shortest distance in which the radar can effectively operate. Closer than this, and the transmitted signal interferes with the reflected signal from target objects. This specification is often far more important than the maximum operating range. After all, if you're a long way from an object it presents little danger, but if you have to pass within a few dozen feet of it you might have a problem.

Electronics Aboard -- By Stephen Fishman

For example, if you're trying to navigate through a channel in the fog and the minimum operating distance of your radar is 30 feet, you have a very real problem if the channel is 50 feet across. In this scenario, your radar would be unable to see any of the channel markers, even if you were traveling down the very center of the waterway.

Output power. A measurement of the maximum potential power output, expressed in kilowatts (kW). Higher peak power translates into a longer range and sharper images on the screen.

Overall noise. The bright area in the center of a radar screen is the result of noise produced by the radar itself. A lower noise measurement produces a smaller bright spot which, in turn, yields more usable viewing area on the screen. A lower noise figure is better than a higher one, and is good or bad relative to other radar units in a given price range.

Bearing accuracy. Most radars produce a relative bearing of displayed objects that is accurate to within plus or minus two degrees and, often, within plus or minus one degree.

Range discrimination. This is a measurement of how far apart two objects have to be before they can be distinguished from each other. For example, if two boats are anchored near one another, a long range discrimination would prevent the radar from separating the two vessels until you were relatively close to them.

Range discrimination is a function of the length of the pulse emitted by the transceiver, with a shorter pulse producing better range discrimination.

Horizontal beam width. This factor also helps determine range discrimination. The beam transmitted by a radar is shaped by its antenna and should be as narrow as possible, since a narrower beam does a better job of differentiating between two objects. As it turns out, a larger antenna creates a narrower beam, which explains why commercial vessels often have eight- or nine-foot antennas.

The problem, though, is that larger antennas produce smaller images on a display. In turn, this means that smaller objects such as buoys or even small boats, may not show up on their screen until the radar-equipped vessel is very close to the object in question.

The cure for this is a very large display, but these are rarely found aboard anything other than military ships and large commercial vessels.

Sidelobe attenuation. This is a measure, expressed in decibels (dB), of the antenna's ability to suppress stray signals that escape to either side of the intended pattern. Sidelobes appear as interference, primarily when looking at large objects.

This rating is similar to the signal-to-noise ratio specification on an audio system and, like a stereo, the lower the number the better. For example, a –20dB is better than a –17dB.

Power & Range

As defined above, maximum range is a function of power and the height of the antenna above the water. Using the example of a radar with a power rating of 2.2kW and a range of 24 nautical miles, the electrical drain is about 45 watts, or a little under 4 amperes. When underway, powerboats constantly recharge their batteries due to an alternator that runs when the engine runs, so the power drain of a radar is never a problem.

For sailboats under sail alone, however, battery drain is always a concern. Most sailboats of any size carry at least two deep cycle batteries with a total minimum capacity of 200 amp-hours, or more. The drain on the ship's batteries is negligible from a 2.2kW radar and, even with other devices drawing 12-volt DC current, a radar of this power could be operated for up to twelve hours without significant impact.

A higher concern for most skippers is the operating range of the radar. A typical 35-foot powerboat with a "radar arch" can mount an antenna about fifteen feet off the water. This yields an effective range for a 2.2kW unit of about 4.5 miles, regardless of whether it's a closed or open array antenna.

Electronics Aboard -- By Stephen Fishman

By contrast, a 35-foot sailboat could locate a radome thirty feet or more off the water, which would yield a 6.5 mile range from the same radar. But this is only half the story.

These numbers are for purposes of comparison only; the actual range will vary depending upon the height of the target.

Most of what you'll see with a radar is not *on* the surface of the water, but rather *above* the surface of the water. Headlands, sailboat masts and antenna arches are all at least several feet above the surface, increasing the effective range of your radar to something close to twice what the numbers might otherwise suggest.

For example, if your radome is mounted on the mast of your 35-foot sailboat at the height of the upper spreader, you should be able to "see" a 35-foot powerboat at a distance of about 11 miles, or a sailboat's reflector at nearly 16 miles. The target is sending back an echo from a reflective surface that is much higher than sea level. As a result, you can see further.

Seeing To Navigate

A radar displays objects on a screen as a result of reflected microwaves sent out from a rotating scanner. But how the information relates to our position and course is up to us to decide. Essentially, there are three methods of using a radar display for navigation; as a heading-up display, as a north-up display or as a course-up display. Each method has its good points and, you will, no doubt, use each method as the occasion dictates.

Heading-Up

This method orients the top of the display with the bow of the boat. This is probably the easiest way of interpreting the information on the screen. Everything you see is relative to the position of the boat and its current direction of movement (heading). If you never use any other method to navigate with a radar, you would most likely never have a problem.

North-Up

This mode is a bit more confusing at first since it orients the display to show objects relative to north, which may or may not parallel your course. This method gives you a sense of how navigation aids on the display move while your boat stays on its intended course. This view might show your vessel moving sideways based on your relative bearing to north, even though you feel the motion is forward.

This method requires an electronic compass to be connected to the radar.

Course-Up

This is the most recently developed method and one that many skippers feel is the most versatile. Course-up mode is possible when a GPS or Loran is connected to the radar. Either unit will orient the display relative to the rhumb line course from your current position to a specific waypoint. If your heading drifts off the intended course due to currents, wind or pilot error, the differential is shown on the screen as cross track error (XTE), which you can then correct. To make a good situation even better, an autopilot is often interfaced with a radar being used in course-up mode.

Typical Features

Almost all radar displays are water-resistant, providing the option of locating the display in an open cockpit or flybridge. With reasonable care, a radar display can be expected to withstand most weather conditions. Beyond that, the display will usually have an electronic bearing line, a variable range marker and a proximity alarm.

Most radar displays for recreational boats are equipped

Electronics Aboard -- By *Stephen Fishman*

with an LCD display that produces sharp images in either monochrome or a color display of up to sixteen colors. Objects on a monochrome display are brighter or less bright depending on the strength of the returning echo. A color display, on the other hand, shows stronger echoes as reds, oranges and yellows and interprets weaker return signals in greens and blues.

This means that the radar interprets stronger returning signals as longer wavelengths and weaker echoes as shorter wavelengths It then displays the various intensities on the screen as a fairly wide range of colors.

Other common features include:

- Zoom capability to enlarge specific areas of the display
- An anti-clutter filter that minimizes echoes from waves along with some atmospheric conditions
- Echo trails that show your most recent course track so you can more easily get a sense of your movement along a course
- An off-center alarm to warn you if cross track error exceeds preset parameters

As you might expect, the more you're willing to spend, the more capabilities and features you get. For most of us, something in the midrange of both cost and complexity is the best compromise. I would highly recommend you seriously consider a radar that permits a GPS and autopilot interface if you plan to spend much time offshore.

Which One

Thanks to micro-electronics, small boat radar has become quite sophisticated, offering features only found on large commercial units as recently as the mid-eighties. The problem now is to strike a balance between simplicity and capability, always being mindful that it's very easy to over do it. In addition to what you feel you can afford to spend, there are

Electronics Aboard -- By Stephen Fishman

a handful of considerations to ponder, all of which directly impact your final selection.

While it's true the smaller the boat, the less space you have available for the antenna and its display, all but the smallest of vessels will have room for a radar. More to the point is the type of craft. Radomes are often the best choice for sailing craft and fishing boats due to the potential tangle of lines with an antenna.

A radome will also be a more appropriate choice for boats as small as twenty feet, regardless of the type of craft.

Transmitter Power

As previously mentioned, power output is stated in kilowatts, with a higher rating producing a longer effective range. I also mentioned that a 4-mile range was the setting used most often – about 95% of the time - by most skippers. More power produces brighter, sharper images on a screen and increases the chances of getting through even the densest fog. But most recreational boaters will find more use for a very short, minimum range than an extended set of long-range "eyes."

On the other hand, if you're crossing oceans or plan to sail out of sight of land most of the time, you'll find higher power and greater range more comforting when it's time to enter an unfamiliar channel or recognize an advancing storm. If this is the your type of boating, chances are you'll want the highest power and the largest antenna you can afford.

Beam Angle

The larger the antenna the narrower the beam angle and the more discriminating the display. A large antenna found on larger radars is more likely to separate objects distinctly that are in close proximity to each other. It will also more clearly define targets such as land masses and inlets.

Electronics Aboard -- By Stephen Fishman

Type Of Display

This is a big one. To review, there are basically two types of screens – a CRT and an LCD. A cathode ray tube (CRT) is sort of like a small television with a monochrome display. It shows bright, high-contrast images and works well in normal light. Unfortunately, a CRT can't be well-sealed against the elements, and it requires quite a bit of space as a result of its shape and size.

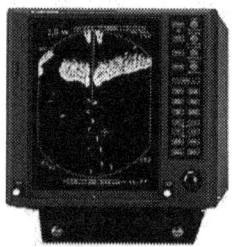

Figure 9-4

CRT display

A liquid crystal display (LCD) is available with either a monochrome or color display, is reasonably waterproof, relatively thin and can be seen easily, even in fairly bright light when it's front-lit or back-lit. In general, LCD displays have a larger viewing area and a flat panel, taking their design primarily from the world of personal computers.

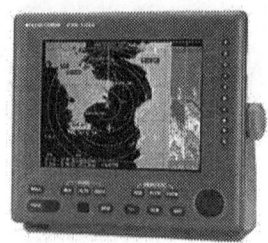

Figure 9-5

LCD color display

Electronics Aboard -- By Stephen Fishman

A LCD is included with all but the most expensive models. This gives the recreational boat exactly what most skippers want – an easy-to-see, relatively inexpensive, compact display.

A monochrome CRT is still the first choice for military and commercial vessels due to the ability of a CRT to deliver sharper, crisper images. There is, however, one notable exception – the PC monitor display.

A few radar suppliers, such as Furuno, have recently begun offering a display borrowed from the world of personal computers. It is a non-interlaced VGA flat-screen color display with a resolution of 640 x 480 pixels. This means you can now use a color radar display that looks familiar, has an even brighter screen than an LCD display and has about the same sharpness as the CRT mentioned earlier.

Some of these newer systems are touted as "black box" technology because all of the components – the transceiver, a keyboard and the display – are housed together and offer more installation options at a lower cost. In addition, standard PC switching devices for monitors can be used, allowing a single monitor to perform double-duty. This cn reduce the number of displays on a flybridge, in a cockpit or at the navigation station in the cabin.

Note: *A complete discussion of display types and their application can be found in Chapter 3.*

Depending on the manufacturer, a radar can offer many unique controls and features to help you navigate more easily, but some features have become somewhat standardized.

Guard Alarm

AKA proximity alarm. A guard alarm alerts you with an audible signal when your boat has reached a predetermined minimum distance, relative to the nearest object. This is a very useful function when you're entering an unfamiliar harbor or navigating in dense fog. The alarm can usually be set either for dead ahead in the direction of travel, or for a 360-degree proximity circle around the vessel.

Target Trails

Also referred to as target tracks. Target trails are a series of echoes that are an afterglow of where a vessel used to be. It's an immediate and unmistakable indication of another boat's direction of movement and general speed. The trail is relative to your boat and can be set from several seconds to several minutes of tracking time.

On a CRT, for example, the target vessel shows up on the screen as a bright green moving object, while the trail is displayed as a dark green, dim image of where the target has been.

VRM

A variable range marker (VRM) is a ring or electronic mark placed on top of any target on the radar display. In most units, an on-screen readout tells you how far away you are from the other object, in nautical miles.

If you're navigating to a specific location, such as a fishing spot or an anchorage area, the VRM can be used in conjunction with an electronic bearing line (EBL). This will not only help plot the distance to the destination, but takes into account drift and cross track error to help you stay more precisely on course.

Cost

This is a topic I hesitate to discuss because whether or not something is affordable is a relative perspective based upon such issues as income, use of the vessel, financial priorities and so forth. So I'll just say this: Radar is one of the most

Electronics Aboard -- *By Stephen Fishman*

expensive navigation tools you can install on your vessel. Depending upon where you go and how often you go there, it can be the single, most secure way of preserving life and limb when the chips are down.

Skippers who have used radar for any length of time invariably agree that among all the electronics and navigation equipment on board, radar would be their first choice if they could have only one device.

Electronics Aboard -- *By Stephen Fishman*

Electronics Aboard -- By Stephen Fishman

Chapter Ten
Loran C

Loran C was one of the first successful electronic navigation systems. The concept of Loran is based on a simple principle, offering sailors the ability to triangulate the position of their vessel by means of multiple broadcast beacons.

Long before GPS was a reality, the navigation system most relied upon by coastal mariners was Loran. Originally introduced as Loran-A - **LO**ng **R**ange **A**id to **N**avigation - for use by the military during World War II, this method of determining a vessel's position didn't become popular with recreational boaters until the late 1970s.

In 1974, the U.S. Coast Guard established Loran-C as the primary civilian navigation system for, what is called the Coastal Confluence Zone (CCZ). The CCZ is an area of navigable water extending from the coastline of the United States to fifty miles offshore, or to the nearest 100-fathom ocean bottom contour line, whichever is furthest. The exceptions to this are the Great Lakes, which are also included and, since the late 1980s, all of the United States' land mass.

Although designed for the CCZ, most Loran signals can travel a lot further than just fifty miles. In fact, under ideal conditions, Loran signals have been used by ships as far as 1,200 miles out to sea. Loran is not confined to just U.S. waters. It covers the Canadian east and west coasts, the North Atlantic, and even parts of Europe, the Mediterranean and Japan.

Electronics Aboard -- By *Stephen Fishman*

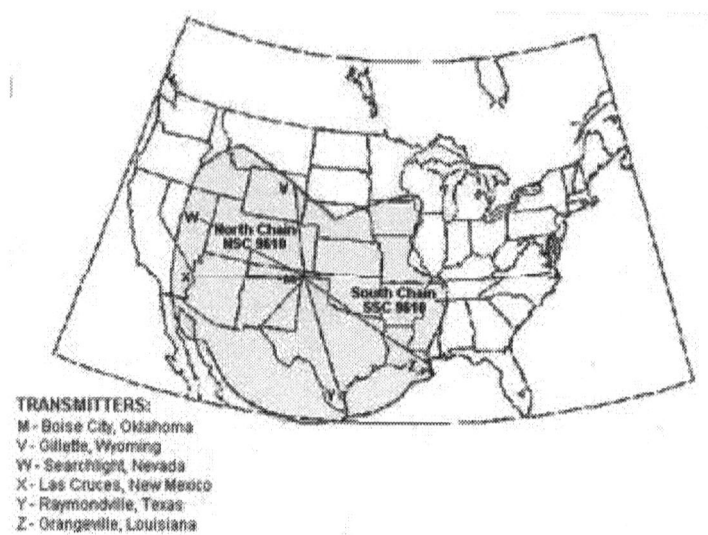

Figure 10-1

U.S. South Central Loran coverage

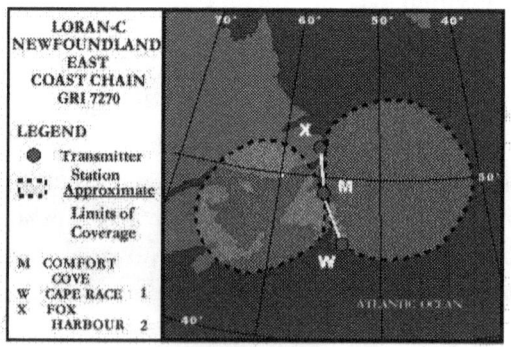

Figure 2

New Foundland and British Columbia Loran coverage

Electronics Aboard -- By Stephen Fishman

How It Works

Imagine sailing or motoring to the middle of a bay. On opposing shores are two foghorns that continually produce short blasts you can easily hear. If you're in the exact middle of the bay between the horns, the volume of their blasts will sound equally loud and the two blasts will seem to hit your ears at the same moment. As you move closer to one of the horns, it will begin to sound louder and the noise will seem to arrive at your location with less delay than the sound coming from the other horn. Eventually, you'll get so close to one of the foghorns that you'll have a hard time hearing the other one.

If you could stop at that moment and measure the time interval between blasts of that distant horn, and knowing the speed of sound, you could calculate how far you were from the source of the sound. Make the same calculation for the sound coming from the nearby foghorn and you can position yourself on a line between them.

Although oversimplified, this is much the same way that Loran fixes the position of your boat. With Loran, however, there are usually three to five sources from which distance data can be gathered, thus providing a way to accurately triangulate a position.

A Loran receiver measures the difference in time between signals sent from a master station, called "M," and two or more secondary stations, commonly referred to as V, W, X, Y, and Z. The time difference (TD) of these 100kHz radio signals is measured in microseconds. When compared to the speed at which the signal travels (about 186,000 miles per second, the speed of light), this shows a significant interval to a Loran receiver.

The signal between a master and one secondary station yields one line of position (LOP). The signal between the master and another secondary station yields an additional LOP. Where these two lines cross is the lat/lon location of the receiver's position aboard a boat. The Loran receiver converts the measured time interval between pulses for a master and two or more secondaries, and converts the data to latitude and longitude.

Although a TD is never measured between two secondary stations, three or more secondaries can increase your confidence in the accuracy of the position fix. Each group of one master station and two to five secondary stations is called a chain, and each chain has a well-defined geographic area of coverage.

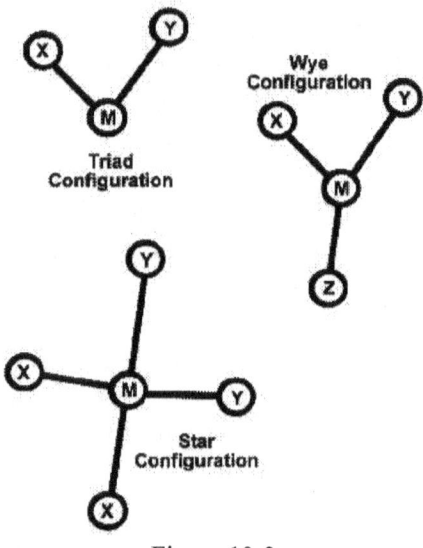

Figure 10-3

Three common chain configurations

The area covered by a Loran chain is so large that only six chains cover the entire United States. Loran chains can be configured to cover areas of different shapes, and this is one of the reasons why so few chains can cover such a large area.

The transmissions from a master station and the secondaries within a chain are offset from each other, so the receiver can more readily distinguish the pulses within a chain. The master station of a chain transmits first and is followed immediately by each secondary station, producing a pattern that is unique to that chain. This is called a group repetition interval (GRI) and is the way in which a Loran receiver identifies which chain it's tuned to. Most receivers automatically select the chain with the strongest signal, but all Loran receivers provide a way for you to enter the GRI for a specific chain. Most Lorans also allow you to store into memory the GRI of several chains.

Not A Straight Fix

The time differences between a master station and a secondary station are not calculated straight lines, but instead are curves called hyperbola. For this reason, Loran navigation is known as hyperbolic navigation.

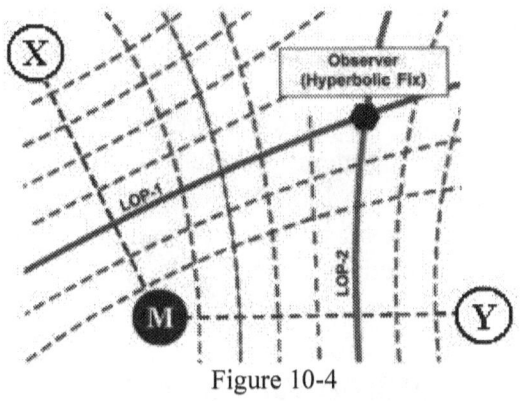

Figure 10-4

A Loran position fix

The U.S. Coast Guard has developed a complex set of mathematical formulas that form the basis of the plane geometry concepts applied to Loran TD measurements and the hyperbolic lines. Personally, I didn't get it when my ninth grade math teacher explained hyperbolas, and I still don't understand it all now. This is one of those things that I take on faith that makes life afloat a little easier. Much in the same way I accept the fact, I don't have to know how an internal combustion

Electronics Aboard -- By *Stephen Fishman*

engine works but I know how to operate a boat under power.

From a theoretical perspective, the point at which two Loran TD lines cross is the intersection of two curved lines. From a practical perspective, sections of these curved lines can be used as straight lines with little error in plotting, as long as you're no closer to a transmitter than twenty nautical miles. This is fairly easy to do considering, that although there are several stations along our coasts, most transmitters are hundreds of miles inland.

Loran TD lines are printed on many charts as a matter of course, and Loran-specific charts are also available. The catch is, on a new fix the Loran navigation system is accurate to no less than one-tenth of a mile (approximately two football fields), with an accuracy of a quarter-mile quite common. On the other hand, once you've plotted a position and stored it in the memory of the Loran receiver, the repeatability of the system should return you to within fifty feet of that previous location.

Harbor charts and charts of other high traffic or restricted areas don't generally include Loran TD lines. For these areas, you'll need to look up and plot the navigation aids in the area and take a fix or two on your position. Once this data has been collected and stored, the Loran's repeatability accuracy can help get you where you need to go.

Automation Is Great

I mentioned that most receivers automatically select the strongest signal and, as a result, decide which chain to lock on to. You can change this selection manually, but I don't recommend it since there are three important issues that must be taken into account, all of which require in-depth knowledge of the Loran navigation system.

First, the configuration of a chain is designed with the goal of creating TD crossing angles that are as close as possible to 90 degrees. This yields the greatest accuracy and, within a chain, the greatest chance of a highly repeatable fix.

Electronics Aboard -- *By Stephen Fishman*

In addition, secondary stations with a tighter gradient are preferred and are automatically selected by the receiver. The gradient refers to how close together the charted spacing is between TD lines from different secondaries within a chain. For example, a TD interval of 5 microseconds could represent one charted nautical mile from one secondary, while the same interval from a different secondary station could represent five miles.

Finally, Loran works best when you're not directly between a master and one of its secondary stations. This location, called a baseline, may prevent acquiring any Loran fix, let alone a good one. The baseline extension – a continuation of the baseline beyond the coverage area of the chain – is one of the factors that the Loran receiver should be programmed to avoid using. Any fixes along the baseline or baseline extension will almost certainly be inaccurate and, in some chains, even impossible to plot.

The bottom line: Let the Loran receiver do the job you paid for it to do – automatic acquisition of a chain and a close approximation of your position.

Obstacles To Accuracy

Loran is susceptible to a variety of factors that degrade the accuracy of a position fix. All are automatically compensated to one degree or another. Some of these conditions can be overcome by entering data manually, but you should be aware of what else can affect your fixes.

The Loran signal can sometimes propagate skyward, bouncing off the ionosphere and returning to earth as skywaves in the same manner as single sideband signals. The groundwave signal – the signal our receivers are designed to capture – offers better accuracy than skywaves, and most receivers are programmed to ignore these delayed reflected signals, even if they happen to be stronger than the groundwave.

The groundwave signal has to pass over either water or land on its way to your receiver, and both surfaces cause a

Electronics Aboard -- By Stephen Fishman

delay of some kind. As you might imagine, signals passing over land are delayed more than signals traveling over water. This is due to the varied topography, ground cover and height variations a signal can encounter. The signal delay factor over water is called a "secondary factor," while the signal delay over land is referred to as an "additional secondary factor," or ASF.

ASF is fairly constant for any area, and an ASF correction is another one of those things programmed into most receivers. You can determine a manual correction by going to a navigation aid that is precisely charted and entering its coordinates. The receiver will measure the difference between its location and the entered coordinates, resulting in a correction factor that can be relied upon for an area of about twenty nautical miles from that spot.

ASF corrections can also be taken from charts, or a document titled *Loran-C Correction Tables* published by the U.S. Defense Mapping Agency.

A storm front between you and the nearest chain can cause problems the receiver isn't designed to handle. Computer-coordinated monitoring stations located in major harbors or heavy traffic areas check signals from masters and secondaries within a chain and make adjustments to the timing sequence. If this should occur, your receiver will display a warning – usually a flashing light of some type – to alert you to the fact that such an event has transpired. Your readings may be acceptably accurate, but it's good practice to check the new readings against old ones if you've been in the area before.

Strong signals on either side of the Loran band can cause problems. Military signals, as well as other strong broadcasts near the Loran band are well-known, and virtually all receivers have "notch filters" that screen out this interference. Interestingly, your receiver will go blank if you do happen to pick up a military broadcast.

Primarily, this is electrical noise that can originate from any one of many sources, including ignition noise and electrical interference from your boat or other vessels up to fifty feet away.

Electronics Aboard -- By *Stephen Fishman*

Fluorescent lights are especially bad, and many manufacturers produce lighting of this type with interference rejection components to help keep them "silent" for Loran reception. If you'd like to test this, tune an AM radio to a setting between stations and listen as you turn a fluorescent fixture on and off. If the static rises and falls significantly in volume, you need a notch filter for your Loran receiver.

Add to the problem, a compliment of navigation instruments that are becoming more sophisticated. Standalone video displays as well as those built into radar, chartplotters and fishfinders use horizontal sweep oscillators. These oscillators can interfere with Loran signals so severely, it can completely negate even a strong Loran signal. Turning each monitor on and off while watching the Loran display will quickly tell you whether or not you have a problem.

If you do have an interference problem, you can eliminate it - or at least minimize it - by making sure both the Loran receiver and the video display are properly grounded. Also try shielding the receiver, to the extent possible, from all video equipment.

Common Features

Manufacturers of Loran-C receivers make every effort to meet, or exceed, all of the requirements specified in the granddaddy of Loran standards, the *Report of Marine Committee No. 70 Radio Technical Commission of Marine Services* (RTCM-70) specification). This document is significant in that it defines the minimum performance standards for a "fully automatic TYPE I receiver." In other words, a Loran-C receiver.

Electronics Aboard -- By Stephen Fishman

Figure 10-5

Furuno LC90 MK2 Loran-C receiver

You should realistically expect to find the following operating features on every Loran receiver, but high-end units will carry more automation and capability.

- Memory storage of all working data at power down
- The ability to store a minimum of 100 waypoints
- Obvious SAVE and GOTO functions
- Steerage to any saved waypoint by using a steering indicator and calculated crosstrack error
- Single, double, or multiple waypoint navigation
- Continuous position display in either Lat/Lon or TD format
- Range and bearing display to any waypoint from the vessel's current position
- Alarms or alerts for waypoint arrival, anchor watch and excessive crosstrack error
- Crosstrack error and the "time-to-go" to the next waypoint
- Average course made good (CMG) and speed over ground (SOG)
- Average velocity made good toward your destination
- A reference number denoting the degree of repeatable accuracy that can be expected
- A digital clock for tracking running time
- Automatic computation of magnetic variation, and the ability to display bearings relative to magnetic north

Electronics Aboard -- By Stephen Fishman

- Extended range operation for fringe areas
- A navigation calculator that can provide a bearing between any two points on earth
- Distance and speed displayed in multiple format options, including nautical miles and knots, kilometers and KPH, or statute miles and MPH.
- Test and performance readouts to check signals and system performance

Additional functionality will increase the price of a Loran-C receiver, but you might want to consider some of these enhancements:

Automatic ASF correction. You might still have to enter a correction manually from time to time but, in my estimation, this should be built into the product. If it's not, move up a model or two to get it.

Automatic GRI selection. Like the ASF correction, I wouldn't purchase a receiver without the ability to select the strongest signal and lock onto that chain.

Storage capacity for 300 waypoints, or more. In your home waters you'll have little use for waypoints, but travel to any new area will change this perspective. It's surprisingly easy to find the need to store a couple of hundred waypoints.

Waypoint return accuracy of fifty feet. The reciprocal course from any new location can be far more relaxing when you know you can hit a previous waypoint within fifty feet or less on the return trip. A more sensitive receiver can increase your confidence in the technology.

A large LCD display. Size alone isn't everything, but it's a good start. Look for a display that has a lot of contrast – as close to black on white as possible – and one that can be easily seen from any angle. A wide viewing angle is especially important for sailboat installations where the helmsman can be as far as fifty degrees off from the center of the display.

Simple front panel controls. You should be able to

Electronics Aboard -- By Stephen Fishman

get a sense of the unit's general operation by the control buttons and their labels.

NMEA0183 data interface. This 4,800 BPS communications port allows the receiver to be connected with other instruments on board.

Although incorporated in many Loran-C receivers, you might want to look for a few more functions that can make life easier for you.

Skywave rejection. This is a built-in feature on most receivers, but check the sales literature to be sure. If this feature is present, there should be an indicator or warning of some type to let you know of possible fix confusion.

Loran chain error indicator. Once again, this is included with most units these days, but ask about this if you don't see it in the product information.

Signal-to-noise readout. This is a relative number that tells you how well the receiver distinguishes between background interference and the signal from a Loran chain.

Low power consumption. This is a consideration whether the unit is a handheld or a fixed-mount receiver.

Flexible mounting options. If the unit is a fixed-mount, there should be several different ways in which the unit can be installed. These should include, overhead, on the surface of the helm, flush-mounted in the helm cabinetry, and so forth. If the unit is a handheld, there should be an optional fixed-mount bracket as well as a pouch or holder.

Price and service. The receiver should have a broad base of service locations and, of course, it should be competitively priced.

Installation

Like any marine receiver, a Loran receiver needs three things to make it work – 12-volts of clean DC power, a good

Electronics Aboard -- By Stephen Fishman

antenna, and a solid ground. Although the first two are relatively easy to accomplish, a good ground can present a challenge.

Since most Loran receivers only draw between 1/2 amp and one amp of power, it's unlikely you'll find your batteries drained as a result of constantly using the Loran. When connecting the receiver, use a minimum of 16-gauge wire, and be sure to wire in a breaker between the battery and the receiver. Ideally, the breaker would be located inside the main power panel along with breakers for other devices, but this is not mandatory.

As a backup against frying your receiver due to a short circuit, install an in-line fuse in the power (red) side of the wire run. Remember, neither the breaker nor the fuse should be rated higher than the amperage draw of the receiver. The result of too large a breaker or fuse is a damaged receiver instead of a blown fuse or tripped breaker.

The groundplane for a Loran receiver is nearly identical in nature and scope to that needed for a single sideband radio. A groundplane of between 60 and 100 square feet is recommended, with components of the system being included for much the same reasons as for an SSB. Groundplane components could include the engine block, keel bolts, and metal through-hulls and may include a copper screen. The link between each component of the groundplane should be copper foil of three to five inches in width.

A complete discussion of the issues surrounding a large groundplane are discussed at length in *Chapter 12: Single Sideband Radios.*

Interestingly, the antenna is the easiest part. Unlike the complex requirements of a single sideband antenna system, the antenna for a Loran receiver is virtually identical to a nine-foot fiberglass CB antenna. In fact, if the antenna should ever break, it can be replaced with most any CB radio antenna fitted with a threaded base of 3/8"–24 in size.

What differentiates the Loran installation from a CB antenna installation is an encapsulated pre-amplifier that

Electronics Aboard -- By *Stephen Fishman*

attaches to the base of the antenna. The pre-amp intensifies the incoming signal and establishes a narrow pass band for the Loran frequency. As with all pre-amps, this one needs electrical power to function, and 12-volt DC power is supplied by the same coaxial cable that sends incoming signals to the receiver.

Another unusual aspect of the antenna installation is that antenna height is of no consequence. All that's required is for the antenna to be clear of obstructions. For a powerboat, the antenna is often mounted on the side of the cabin. Many sailboats will find the best location to be the stern rail or an aft corner of the deck.

There are two critical considerations, however. The antenna should be as vertical as possible even though the precise angle is unimportant, and the antenna should be located as far as possible from any device that produces electrical noise. Examples of this type of device are refrigeration systems and air conditioning compressors, bait tank motors and fluorescent lights.

If It Doesn't Work

If your receiver works fine everywhere you go except one or two places, chances are it's the result of a strong military signal. Your local dealer should be aware of these types of problems and be able to install notch filters to resolve the issue.

On the other hand, if your receiver works well under sail but not power, it's a good bet you need to install a noise suppressor on the ignition. Because most boats have many potential conflicts of this nature, your local chandlery should be able to supply just about any type of noise suppression necessary.

As with any other electrical device, solid connections are absolutely essential for trouble-free operation. Regularly check connection tightness and for signs of corrosion. You must repair or replace fittings as needed.

Electronics Aboard -- *By Stephen Fishman*

In Case You Were Wondering

Even with all the attention given to Loran-C in the past few years from manufacturers offering new makes and models, Loran will likely be displaced by GPS in the not-too-distant future. With the introduction of WAAS error correction, differential GPS has become routinely accurate within less than ten feet. This is quite different from the fifty-foot accuracy expectations of Loran to return to a previous position fix.

Even so, until Loran is discontinued, the United States, along with many foreign countries, will continue to make Loran a viable navigation option.

Electronics Aboard -- *By Stephen Fishman*

Electronics Aboard -- By Stephen Fishman

Chapter Eleven
GPS

The Global Positioning System is a network of 24 satellites that circle the Earth in six different paths, making a complete orbit in just under 12 hours. Speed freaks might be thrilled - that's more than 5,400 miles per hour! The first GPS satellite - often referred to as a NAVSTAR satellite - was launched in February of 1978, but the Department of Defense didn't declare the GPS system to be totally operational until 1995.

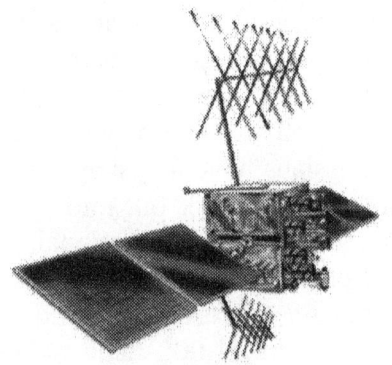

Figure 11-1

GPS satellite

Each satellite weighs about 2,000 pounds and is approximately 17 feet across, including extended solar panels that generate 1100 watts of power. Each satellite transmits two simultaneous signals - L1, for civilians and L2 for the military – at a paltry 50 watts.

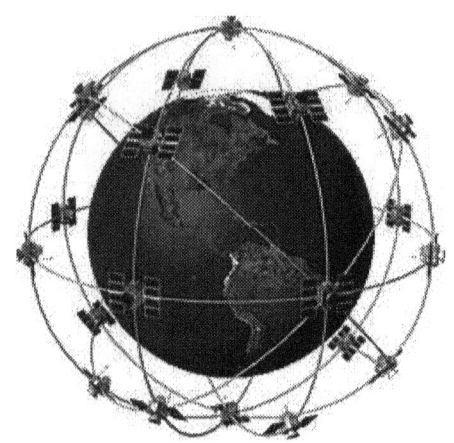

Figure 11-2

GPS network

The life expectancy of a NAVSTAR satellite is about 10 years – a long time in satellite years, and about 2 years in human years - which is why replacements are continually being built and launched. The entire 24 satellite GPS constellation cost about $12 billion to build and launch into orbit. Interestingly, the Russians have a system – named GLONASS - that is identical to the network put into space by the United States but it's not yet completely operational.

The orbital paths of GPS satellites are confined to the space between about 60 degrees North and 60 degrees South latitudes, at an altitude of 11,000 nautical miles. This means you can receive GPS signals anywhere in the world, any time of the year. You can even sail to the poles and still pick up the signal from GPS satellites.

The GPS network works in all kinds of weather, which is its single greatest advantage over land-based Loran-C and celestial navigation.

Electronics Aboard -- By Stephen Fishman

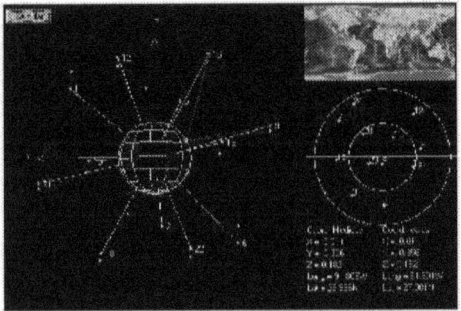

Figure 11-3

Relative orbits of satellites

How It Works

The GPS signal contains three types of information – a pseudo-random code, ephemeris data and almanac data. The pseudo-random code identifies the satellite sending the signal and can be any number between 1 and 32. This ID number, called a PRN – *P*seudo-*R*andom *N*umber - is the number displayed on a GPS receiver that tells you which satellite signal is being received. The numbering system is intended to simplify maintenance of the network by providing a way for as many as 32 satellites to be in orbit while only 24 are actually "working." This allows one or more replacement satellites to be launched and turned on before actually turning off the older ones.

Ephemeris data contains critical information, such as the status of the satellite along with the current date and time. Since elapsed time is one aspect of a fix calculation, this part of a transmission is essential for determining a position.

The almanac data tells the GPS receiver where each NAVSTAR satellite should be at any given time. Each satellite transmits almanac data describing orbital information for itself, as well as for all other satellites in the network.

Each satellite transmits a message that tells your GPS receiver the ID number of the satellite, its position at the time of the transmission, and the time and date of the transmission.

Electronics Aboard -- By Stephen Fishman

The GPS receiver processes the information, saves it and makes the data available for continual use by the receiver. Among other things, this data can be used to set - or reset - the receiver's internal clock. This is an over oversimplification of what happens, but you get the idea.

The Fix

A GPS receiver subtracts the time that a signal was transmitted by a satellite from the time the signal was received by your GPS. The amount of time difference tells the GPS receiver how far away that particular satellite is by using this formula:

(signal transmission speed) x (measured time interval) = distance traveled

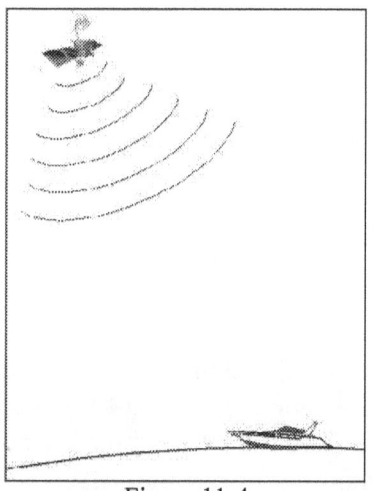

Figure 11-4

Single broadcasting satellite

If we have distance calculations from at least two more satellites, the GPS receiver can triangulate your position. With a minimum of three satellites, your receiver can determine a latitude and longitude position, called a 2D position fix. With four or more satellites, your GPS can come up with a 3D position fix that includes altitude as well as latitude and longitude. By continuously updating your position, the GPS can also calculate your speed – known as *speed over ground* (SOG) - and your direction of travel, referred to as *ground track*.

Note: *In its simplest form, a GPS can act as a compass but, in order to accomplish this most basic of all navigation tasks, it must be in motion. In other words, don't unpack your new GPS receiver and expect it to display an electronic representation of a compass while you're sitting on your porch at home.*

One factor affecting GPS accuracy is something called satellite geometry. This refers to the location of satellites relative to each other as seen from the position of your GPS receiver. For example, if your GPS has locked onto – acquired - three satellites and all three are in the sky to the northwest of your position, satellite geometry is considered to be poor. This is due to the fact that they are all providing measurements from the same general direction.

In times past, this was a rather common occurrence since there were fewer satellites in orbit. The result of poor geometry is poor triangulation and inaccurate positioning. In fact, poor satellite geometry can produce a positioning error of as much as 500 feet. Today, however, this is an unlikely scenario due to two significant improvements in the global positioning system: First, there are more satellites currently in use by the GPS network. Second, most models of GPS receivers can now acquire a minimum of eight satellites, with a twelve satellite lock-on not uncommon.

Returning to our three satellite network. If those same three satellites are spread out in different directions relative to the location of our GPS, the accuracy of all functions will improve dramatically.

Electronics Aboard -- By *Stephen Fishman*

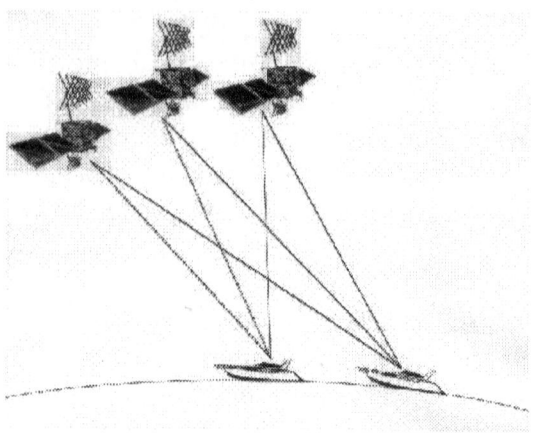

Figure 11-5

Poor satellite geometry

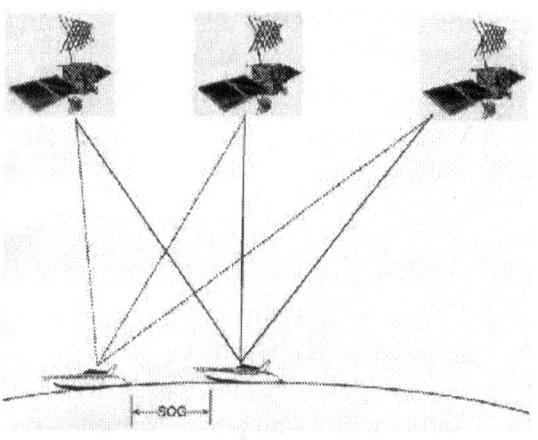

Figure 11-6

Good satellite geometry

    The further apart these satellites are separated, up to a maximum of about 90 degrees - north, east and west, for example – the more satellite geometry improves. The area where all three signals intersect is more diverse when this situation is established. This results in a potential inaccuracy of less than 100 feet. Even this error has decreased dramatically

Electronics Aboard -- *By Stephen Fishman*

with the discontinuance of selective availability.

Until May, 2000, selective availability (SA) was a U.S. government-sponsored electronic error introduced into GPS satellite transmissions. It was intended to make it more difficult for hostile governments to pinpoint the locations of our ships, military bases and cities. The U.S. military, of course, used decoders to strip out the induced error in order to take full advantage of what the GPS network had to offer for position accuracy.

With the absence of SA, recreational boaters can now expect even a moderately-priced GPS receiver to provide positioning information, as well as other data, that is accurate to within less than about 15 feet under ideal circumstances.

All of this applies to any GPS receiver, whether it is used for marine navigation, on land or for aviation. If you happen to be one of those people who hate to stop and ask directions, one of the new automobile GPS map systems may be just the thing for you. But beware that tall buildings can block the signal so you may not get the performance you expect in a dense urban area.

The same applies for hikers and backpackers. As more of the sky is obstructed by terrain such as canyons and mountains, acquiring a position fix becomes increasingly more difficult. For this reason, some receivers are designed to tell you where in the sky the satellites are located by providing their azimuth and elevation.

Another type of GPS reception error is called multipath. Multipath occurs when a radio signal is reflected off an object before it is "seen" by the receiver. Multipath is what causes a ghost image on a television that uses "rabbit ears," a VHF "loop" antenna or even a marine television antenna hoisted into the rigging of a sailboat. The ghosting problem is less common these days with the widespread use of cable and satellite TV dishes, but if you've got an old style antenna you're going to get old style reception.

Although not typically an issue in marine applications, multipath can occur when a signal bounces off a building or a

Electronics Aboard -- By *Stephen Fishman*

mountain before reaching the antenna of the GPS receiver. Since the signal takes longer to reach the antenna than if it traveled in a direct path, the GPS receiver thinks the satellite is farther away than it is. This adds an error of something less than 15 feet to the position calculation. Certainly not a big deal if you're on land unless, of course, you happen to have fallen down a well or crevasse.

Other sources of error can include internal clock errors and a nifty atmospheric problem called propagation delay. A GPS receiver is designed to compensate for these effects, too, but minor errors can, and still do occur.

Note: *Propagation delay is the result of the GPS signal slowing down as it passes through the upper layers of the Earth's atmosphere.*

Accuracy

A moderately priced marine GPS receiver can generally provide accuracy to within 50 feet, depending on the number of satellites available and their geometry at the time. More sophisticated and expensive GPS receivers – we're talking thousands here - can get within a centimeter of a given point by using multiple GPS frequencies. However, a typical marine GPS receiver's accuracy can be improved to fifteen feet - or in some cases less than ten feet – with the addition of Differential GPS (DGPS).

DGPS

DGPS uses a second receiver to compute corrections to GPS satellite measurements. Corrections are available through several services, both free or by subscription, that provide DGPS corrections. The U.S. Coast Guard and the U.S. Army Corps of Engineers transmit DGPS corrections by means of marine beacon stations that operate in the 283.5 - 325.0 kHz frequency range and are free of charge. The only

Electronics Aboard -- By Stephen Fishman

catch is, you have to buy a DGPS beacon receiver. The beacon receiver is coupled to your GPS receiver via a three-wire connection, which relays the corrections in a standard serial data format called *RTCM SC-104*.

Subscription DGPS services are available on FM radio station frequencies or via satellite. In either case, you'll still need at least another receiver to pick up these transmissions and then send them to your GPS receiver.

DGPS is one of the reasons why the Department of Defense discontinued selective availability. After all, if you can buy a DGPS receiver and fix your position within a few yards, so can a hostile government or a fanatic terrorist. In the meantime, SA was just making it hard on honest folk like you and me.

Navigation Vocabulary

No matter what you do, from playing chess to crossing oceans, every activity has its own terminology, acronyms and phrases. Now that you know how the GPS network works, it's time to take a look at some of the more common terms that help you use the features a GPS has to offer. A more complete list can be found in the Appendix.

Bearing (BRG) - The compass direction from your current position to a destination. This function can be used to help get you to a marina entrance, another vessel or the nearest coastal restaurant.

Heading - Your direction of movement, taking into consideration such issues as winds, currents, sea conditions, etc.

Course - Your general direction of travel from the beginning of a journey to its destination.

Route - A planned course of travel, divided into legs, that has been defined by a series of waypoints. For example, a trip from Galveston Island to Brownsville, Texas might be

Electronics Aboard -- *By Stephen Fishman*

defined with waypoints at Port Aransas and Corpus Christi. It could also be defined by a series of waypoints that closely approximate the positions of several offshore oil rigs in the Gulf of Mexico.

Waypoint - A named position along a route that has been stored in the memory of the GPS. Typically, waypoints are determined by reviewing a series of charts of the intended route and storing them prior to the start of a trip. A waypoint can also be entered into memory by placing the GPS receiver at the location of the waypoint. This works well for waypoints that are used repeatedly, such as a channel marker or harbor entrance.

Leg - A segment of a route measured from one waypoint to another. A leg can be as short as the distance from one channel marker to another, or as far apart as two villages on opposite coasts of the same ocean.

GOTO - A course with only one leg that begins at your current position and ends at a predefined waypoint. Calculating a GOTO is a good to know when a seasick crew turns mutinous because the captain refuses to return to port in heavy weather.

Desired track - The plotted compass course you intend to travel. This is not always the course you actually travel because sea conditions can change unexpectedly.

Crosstrack error (XTE) The distance you are off your desired course. For the cause of this condition, see *Desired Track*.

Estimated time enroute (ETE) - The time remaining to the destination provided the vessel's speed and course are maintained.

Estimated time of arrival (ETA) - The time at which shore leave begins.

Initialization - The first time a GPS receiver orients itself to its current position. This occurs each time a GPS is turned on. Once initialized, the receiver can acquire satellites and calculate a changing position quickly.

Man Over Board (MOB) - A button on virtually

every GPS that instantly inputs a waypoint, and calculates the steering guidance needed to bring the vessel back to this position. With luck, this will never happen or, if it does, you will be so close to the victim that steering guidance will be unnecessary.

Velocity Made Good (VMG) - The speed at which the vessel is approaching the destination, based upon its current speed and course.

Speed Over Ground (SOG) - The rate at which a vessel is traveling across the bottom, irrespective of the destination. You could be making great headway through the water but not actually making progress towards your destination. You may be way off course or fighting a hard running tide.

Course Over Ground (COG) - Your actual course that has been corrected for winds and currents. This information is accurate only if you have previously entered into the memory of the GPS the speed and direction of wind and currents.

The Hardware

Like VHF marine radios, GPS receivers are available in two versions – handheld and fixed-mount - and the considerations regarding which type to choose are much the same.

A fixed-mount receiver will invariably have a remote antenna resembling a mushroom, that is connected to the receiver with a cable of up to fifty feet. On a sailboat, the antenna is commonly mounted on the stern rail. Larger vessels may have an antenna mast or radar arch near the stern that carries all of the ship's antennas. On a motoryacht, the GPS antenna may be mounted on top of the flybridge arch along with other antennas often grouped in this location.

A handheld unit has a built-in antenna, but many models have external antennas available.

One of the interesting things about a GPS antenna is

Electronics Aboard -- By Stephen Fishman

that it doesn't have to have an unobstructed view of the sky. For example, a GPS antenna can "see" through a canvas bimini or a vinyl shade over a flybridge. Even so, most marine installations place a GPS antenna in an exposed area in an effort to reduce multipath error, mentioned earlier.

Similar to VHF, it's a good idea to carry both a fixed-mount and a handheld GPS receiver if you plan to be out of sight of land for an extended period of time. If your ship's batteries fail, the handheld unit may be your fastest way out of trouble. This scenario presupposes one of two situations. First, you had the foresight to enter into the handheld receiver, all of the waypoints you entered into the fixed-mount unit. Second, you have updated the handheld with position data as the journey unfolds. Without one of these two plans, you may have a problem even though you have a back-up GPS.

Safety First

There is one fundamental aspect of navigation that needs to be mentioned here. Whether you're using a GPS, a chartplotter or a notebook computer with electronic charts, you need a backup that isn't electronic, doesn't rely on electricity, doesn't depend upon an external source for position data, and that you absolutely KNOW will be there.

The only items to fit the bill are a compass and set of paper charts.

Paper charts are considered by many boaters to be old-fashioned and cumbersome when compared to the ease of pushing buttons on a device the size of a paperback novel. Batteries DO fail and external sources of information are sometimes inaccurate, even when it comes from the United States government.

If you plot your position on a paper chart as you sail away into the sunset, you'll have a reliable starting point to rescue yourself in case all your gadgets crater at the same time. At a minimum, a paper chart provides you with a souvenir of the trip and proof that you really did go there and do that, even

Electronics Aboard -- By Stephen Fishman

if the journey was blissfully uneventful.

As for a compass, any boat over twelve feet in length is likely to have had a compass supplied as standard equipment. Do yourself a favor and learn how to use it either on a do-it-yourself basis, or by attending a course sponsored by organizations such as the U.S. Power Squadron, the YMCA, or the Parks and Wildlife Department. You will quickly discover that the toughest part about using a compass is learning how to compensate for deviation and the proximity of ferrous metals.

In general, a GPS is a fairly rugged, highly reliable piece of equipment. But you never know.

The Datum

I know it's hard to believe, but not all charts show the same information. They are all very close to the same, but they're not *exactly* the same, which is why there are at least three map designation standards that boaters should know. Not all GPS makes and models contain the same number of choices when it comes to datum. For example, most Garmin units contain just over a hundred datum settings while Eagle/Lowrence units are equipped with nearly two hundred.

All charts are drawn to a standard that includes latitude and longitude positions for specific measured locations. Your GPS should always be "tuned" to the setting shown on the chart in use. This is an easy change to make on a GPS receiver and the user's manual will, invariably, have instructions for accomplishing this task.

Most marine charts for waters around the United States and Canada are drawn to either North American Datum (NAD) 27, NAD 83 or WSG 84 standards, with the higher number indicating a newer chart. NAD 83 and WSG 84 are close to the same, but no two datum will provide precisely the same reading; there will always be a difference of a few minutes of distance.

In contrast, there are hundreds of other datum settings

for other parts of the world, including Australian Geodetic 84 for example. The chart you're referencing will always tell you which setting to use.

Go To Where

One of the most useful functions of a GPS is the GOTO function. If you're a fisherman, you can easily imagine how cool it would be to reliably return to a great fishing spot time after time. If something valuable accidentally goes overboard, entering the position in a GPS will lead you back to the same place the next day with diving gear and crew.

The slick thing about the GOTO function is you don't have to start out from the same place each time. If you're that fisherman I mentioned, you might leave from one boat ramp this weekend and another ramp the next time. If you're going to dive for that lost treasure, the dive boat may be launched from a different marina than where your boat is slipped. In both instances, activating the GOTO function will display the position that was saved into memory and you will be shown what course to take to get back to that spot.

Bear in mind that the GOTO function is blind. It has no knowledge of obstacles; it only knows the most direct route to the GOTO destination. Even on the water, it's not unusual to find you can't take the most direct course to get where you want to be. Channels, points of land, submerged objects and other boaters may all have to be circumvented.

Taking A Trip

As mentioned before, a GPS may be smart enough to know where it's located on the face of the earth, but a GPS is blind to obstacles between your current position and where you want to go. As a result, a route will never be a straight line, but rather a group of legs that zig and zag, eventually taking you to your destination. When you're sitting back in your easy chair in

Electronics Aboard -- By Stephen Fishman

front of a nice warm fire, dreaming about your vacation of a lifetime, don't forget that your trip will almost certainly require more time and distance than you first suppose. It's quite common for a journey across the water to be as much as 50% longer than what may appear on a chart.

A GPS receiver can store dozens, and in many models even hundreds, of waypoints which simplifies the task of planning a trip of almost any length. If you were to open a chart and trace your route from the starting point to the destination, you will, invariably, find places along the way that are natural reference points. These might include coastal towns, restaurants, fuel docks, boatyards, lighthouses, bridges or simply points of interest along the way. In each case, these points represent potential waypoints on your journey that can be identified on a chart by their latitude/longitude position. If you want, these stops could be stored in the memory of your GPS and used as waypoints along your route.

After you've decided where you want to go, the next step is to look at a nautical chart and plan your route. Route planning takes one of two forms, either a point-to-point journey or a nonstop passage.

A point-to-point journey is one in which you sail from one place to another along a predetermined path until you reach your destination, taking time to see what there is to see along the way. A nonstop open water passage, although certainly a romantic notion of the ultimate seafarer, is something few of us are intrepid enough to do. Even so, both types of trips have one thing in common: they both navigate using a series of predetermined waypoints.

The coastal sailor navigates by putting into port each evening at a waypoint that is a marina or other safe anchorage. The passagemaker is guided by waypoints designated by offshore rigs, heading changes in shipping lanes or coastal landmarks such as lighthouses. Whichever you choose, a GPS can make short work of keeping track of each waypoint or stop along your way.

Electronics Aboard -- By Stephen Fishman

The Ultimate Convenience

Whether you're using a handheld GPS or a fixed mount unit, no doubt the ultimate in navigating along a route is achieved when you can download your waypoint data to an autopilot. The GPS knows where to go and continually feeds this information to the autopilot which, in turn, steers where the GPS tells it to go. You can't exactly sit back and do nothing, but the combination is awesome and has the potential to provide the most carefree, relaxing journey you're ever likely to make.

All but the most basic of GPS receivers can be connected to an electronic autopilot and most are equipped from the manufacturer with the appropriate cable. If you plan ahead a bit, you might find the best bargain is a system offered by a single vendor that includes a GPS, an autopilot, a wind speed/direction transducer and perhaps even radar. When all of your electronics are supplied by a single supplier, they will usually work together more seamlessly and interconnect more easily.

Satellite Signal Correction

Many manufacturers, including Garmin and Ratheon, now offer GPS receivers that take advantage of a new satellite signal correction system designed to improve the accuracy and integrity of all GPS signals, including differential GPS enhancements. Currently, there are three separate, but compatible, systems being developed that are either in operation now or soon will be:

• Wide Area Augmentation System (WAAS), developed by the Federal Aviation Administration (FAA) in the U.S.
• European Geo-stationary Navigation Overlay System (EGNOS), still under development by a European consortium
• The MTSAT Satellite-Based Augmentation System (MSAS),

being developed by the Japanese Civil Aviation Bureau (JCAB) for civil aviation use of these systems, the WAAS system is the most advanced, covers the largest area, and includes the entire United States, in addition to a large areas outside of this country.

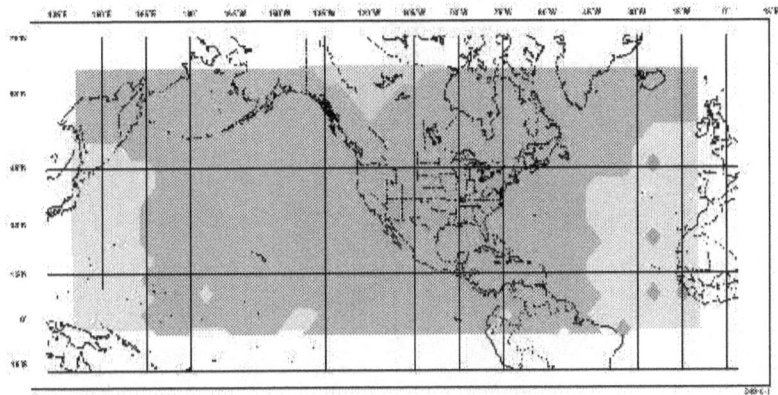

Figure 11-7

WAAS coverage map

The combination of the WAAS, EGNOS and MSAS systems will eventually provide global satellite-based differential GPS augmentation which will continue into the future.

How WAAS Works

WAAS is comprised of three primary components:

- Ground reference stations in multiple locations across the United States
- Master stations located on the east and west coasts
- Geo-stationary satellites located above the equator

The ground reference stations are located at plotted positions and receive data continuously from GPS orbiting satellites. The ground reference stations send their data to master stations that calculate the error of the GPS-received positions and generate corrected data. The corrected "differential" signals are sent to two geo-stationary satellites which, in turn, broadcast corrected data on standard GPS frequencies. Recently developed GPS receivers, such as the Raystar 120, can use corrected data transmitted by the geo-stationary satellites to reduce navigation error to a maximum of 10 feet and, in ideal conditions, no more three feet.

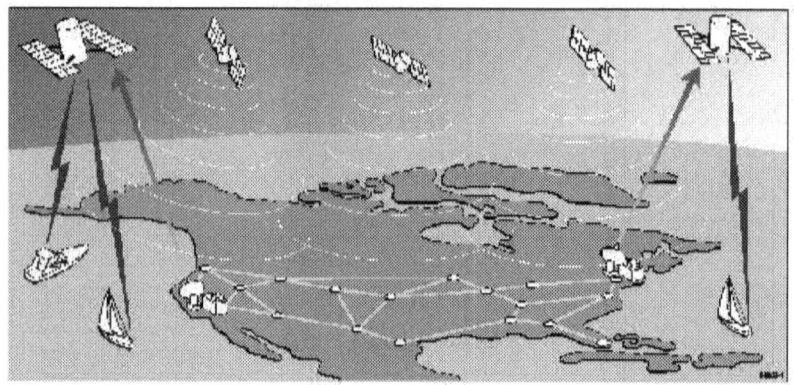

Figure 11-8

WAAS system

The WAAS system was originally developed by the FAA with aviation in mind, and the agency is still testing the system for aviation use. WAAS is expected to be certified by the FAA sometime in 2002. Beware. During the testing and certification period, continuous WAAS service is expected, but you should be prepared for the possibility of brief signal outages as refinements and upgrades are made to the system. In other words, don't completely rely on this new system, yet. The status of WAAS and planned outages are available on-line at Raytheon's web site http://www.raytheontands.com/waas.

Electronics Aboard -- By Stephen Fishman

Chapter Twelve
Single Sideband Radios

In 1914, it was determined, from a purely theoretical perspective, a modulated radio wave is made up of two sidebands and a carrier signal. A year later, an inventor named John Carson – no relation to the famous late night guest show host – applied this concept to a new idea. His position was; if you suppress one of the sidebands as well as the carrier wave, radio signals could be transmitted further with far less power than most people thought possible.

It took him eight years, but in 1923 he was finally granted a patent and made the first transatlantic radio broadcast using his new-fangled idea of a single sideband (SSB). The antennas of the time could only handle a limited bandwidth and the available power sources were rather limited in what they could generate. Even so, the demonstration was a success. By 1927, transatlantic radio transmission capabilities were made available to the general public.

This sounds pretty good, but all of the effort at the time was still only in the low-frequency bands where potential range and power was limited. All that changed with World War II and the intense need for the best communications possible. Since then, virtually all SSB activity has been focused in the high-frequency portion of the radio band.

Today, SSB is used primarily for ship-to-ship and ship-to-shore communications over distances not possible with other types of radios, including marine VHF. Depending upon the time of day, the weather conditions and your choice of

Electronics Aboard -- By Stephen Fishman

radio frequencies, single sideband can provide communications on a global scale.

In 1971, the FCC expanded marine VHF service primarily as a means of local communication on the water. They also phased in single sideband as the preferred method of long-distance communication on the water.

The Signal

A single sideband signal concentrates your voice into a radio wave capable of traveling thousands of miles. This compressed, highly efficient broadcast eliminates the lower sideband and carrier wave portion of the waveform. In the process, it acquires a more powerful signal. By comparison, a commercial AM radio broadcast sends out a duplicate voice waveform, along with a carrier signal, whose sole job is to quiet background noise when nothing else is going on. Since a single sideband has only one sideband with no carrier or mirror-image wave, all of the power the radio can muster is focused on transmitting your voice as clearly and as far as possible.

There is virtually no battery drain when you're not broadcasting. When you do broadcast, the system "relaxes" between words. This makes SSB an especially wise choice for long-range communications aboard sailing vessels and other boats with limited battery capacity.

The transmitted signal is compacted into a very narrow bandwidth, allowing receivers to filter out nearly half of the normal noise level. The FCC mandates very close tolerances be maintained regarding the precision of SSB frequencies.

Most people now use a control known as a "clarifier." A rather recent enhancement to single sideband, a clarifier, produces normal sounding voice reception even when the signal originates from great distances. This wasn't always the case. For many years, everyone's voice sounded like an intentional imitation of Mickey Mouse.

Electronics Aboard -- By Stephen Fishman

Frequencies

A single sideband transceiver can broadcast on any one of eight bands, including 2MHz, 4MHz, 6MHz, 8MHz, 12MHz, 16MHz, 22MHz, and 25MHz. Each frequency has a different range during the day than at night. This aspect of operation changes as the frequency gets higher.

The 2MHz and 4MHz bands are most commonly used for coastal communications and are often referred to as "local" frequencies. These medium-range frequencies are just beyond the range of VHF and provide a range of about 1,000 miles at night but only about 100 miles during the day.

All frequencies between 6MHz and 25MHz are typically grouped together and known collectively as "high-seas" frequencies due to their extended ranges. Each is assigned a channel designation. In 1991, all of the high-seas channels were assigned new frequencies by the FCC.

6MHz and 8MHz provide good local communications during the day with a range of about 600 miles, but really reach out at night where broadcast ranges can extend to as much as 3,000 miles. Historically, the 6MHz band was most commonly found only on the Mississippi River, but that isn't the case today.

The higher frequencies – 12MHz, 16MHz and 22MHz – are considered "worldwide" frequencies. The 12MHz and 16MHz bands have a nighttime global range when you're broadcasting in the direction of the sun, but a reduced range of no more than 3,000 miles during the day.

One of the highest frequencies, 22MHz, is just the opposite. Its worldwide capabilities exist only during the day; at night, its range is seriously curtailed.

Two Waves

There are two waveforms in every SSB broadcast, a groundwave and a skywave. A groundwave skims the surface

Electronics Aboard -- *By Stephen Fishman*

of the water and can travel up to 200 miles, but is normally limited to a range of about 100 miles. The groundwave makes the connection between a boat and a land-based station, making the groundwave the functional equivalent of a "local" high-seas broadcast. A groundwave is primarily dependent upon a strong signal and little else to reach a receiver, but a groundwave can be interrupted by weather conditions such as thunderstorms, waterspouts and strong winds.

The other waveform in a sideband signal is called a skywave. Skywaves bounce off the underside of the ionosphere and are reflected back to the surface, often thousands of miles away.

As you may remember from seventh grade science class, the ionosphere is a multilayered stratified area of ionized gas and microscopic particles that envelope the entire earth. The height of the ionosphere above the surface, its ion density and its refraction capabilities are all affected by the sun's radiation. This means these qualities are different during the day than they are at night. In addition, the height, density and refraction of the ionosphere is affected by the changing of seasons as well as an eleven-year solar cycle.

The lower frequencies – 2MHz through 8MHz – are shorter wavelengths and bounce back to earth over shorter distances. The higher frequencies - 12MHz to 22MHz - are longer wavelengths and return to the surface after having traveled significant distances. For example, it's not unusual to be able to talk to someone in Italy while you're in San Diego harbor. If conditions in the ionosphere are strong and sufficiently dense, a second bounce can take your transmission twice the expected distance. This second bounce produces the range for which SSB is best known.

Electronics Aboard -- *By Stephen Fishman*

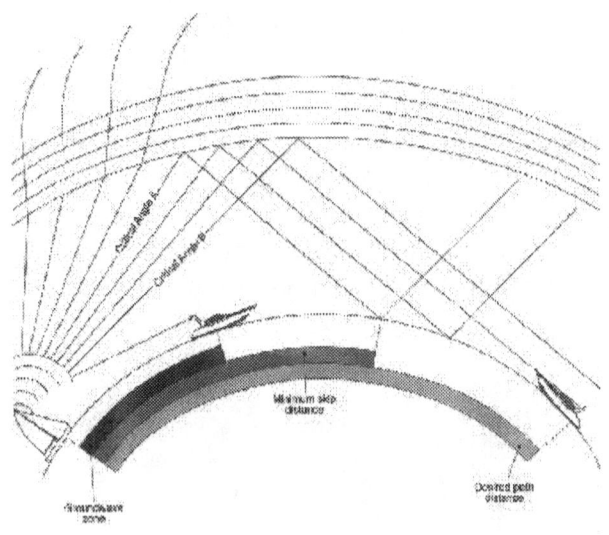

Figure 12-1

Skywave reflections

In general, the ionosphere increases in altitude above the earth and becomes denser during daylight hours. At night, it becomes less dense and settles to a lower altitude. This cycle of daytime warming and altitude change is the primary reason for changes in broadcast ranges from daytime to nighttime. Unlike groundwaves, skywaves aren't affected by changes in local weather but, instead, are affected only by changes in the ionosphere.

If you want to increase the range of your transmission, switch to a higher frequency but beware that a higher frequency can sometimes be the cause of communications problems. For example, if you wanted to talk to someone aboard another boat within visual range, a high frequency would skip over their boat and they would never hear you. Higher frequencies use a longer wavelength, so the "skip" distance – the distance between bounces – could easily miss their antenna. For this type of "local" call, use a lower frequency to make sure their antenna can pick up the signal.

Electronics Aboard -- *By Stephen Fishman*

The Hardware

Marine single sideband is similar to marine VHF in that it's comprised of a transceiver and an antenna. In addition, a SSB set also includes an antenna coupler located in line between the radio and the antenna. A coupler, also called a tuner, provides access to frequency channels on all eight SSB bands instead of limiting the radio's use to only one band.

Figure 12-2

Typical SSB

The Paperwork

The FCC has two basic requirements for single sideband radios. First, unlike a marine VHF radio, the FCC requires you to apply for, and obtain, a ship's station license for a single sideband radio. The assigned call letters must then be used when transmitting or receiving a broadcast. If you're one of the older crowd who was granted a ship's station license when the FCC still required one for a marine VHF radio, you'll use the same call letters for your SSB.

Second, you must have a permanently installed marine VHF radio before you can legally install and use a single sideband radio on your boat.

Note: *A handheld VHF radio doesn't satisfy this FCC requirement. The radio must be a fixed-mount unit.*

It's the government's position that you should use a marine VHF radio when possible for local communication, since the frequencies assigned to SSB use are more limited and potentially more crowded.

Ham Radio

A single sideband radio can typically recieve ham radio signals. Ham broadcasts are high-frequency transmissions that, like SSB, are well-known for their extended range. At sea, it's not uncommon to pick up the BBC in Great Britain as well as other foreign radio broadcasts. You don't need a license to listen in to these broadcasts but you do need a ham radio license to transmit. A ham radio license is only obtainable with effort, and you must be willing to apply yourself to the study demanded in order to qualify for a ham radio license. Personally, it's not for me. Between a marine VHF and SSB, I've got all the communication capabilities I need.

When You Need Help

If you encounter an emergency situation or, worse, find yourself in an emergency situation, all bets are off. Get on the radio – VHF, SSB, ham, tin cans tied together with a string, anything - and let everyone in listening range know you need help. If you broadcast on single sideband or ham frequencies without a license you'll eventually run afoul of the FCC, but in the event of an emergency all officiousness is set aside. When this occurs, no one cares about anything other than where you are and your current situation.

The U.S. Coast Guard, along with other distress-related agencies around the world, routinely monitors 2,182 kHz, located within the 2MHz band. This provides a fast way to contact thousands of coastal and near-shore listeners 24-hours a day, seven days a week should you need help when VHF distress channel 16 isn't enough.

In an effort to provide longer-range help to mariners, the U.S. Coast Guard also monitors five additional channels –

Electronics Aboard -- By Stephen Fishman

424, 601, 816, 1205 and 1625 – as a part of their AMVER system, the Automated Mutual-Assistance Vessel Rescue program. With this network, the Coast Guard can identify the position of military and commercial ships in the area of an emergency, and can signal them to change course and render assistance.

Staying Connected

A single sideband radio provides access to land-based telephone operators who can connect you to anyone with a telephone. These calls aren't cheap, but it's a good example of how an SSB can help keep you in touch with the rest of the world.

The same people that can connect you to family and friends offer other services. Many of these companies maintain what are called "traffic lists," a sort of delayed call waiting, that lets ships at sea know they have calls from shore-side. Operators can also patch you through to rescue centers, hospitals and other medical centers - at no cost.

Every four hours, shore-side marine telephone operators broadcast weather reports, storm warnings and other safety information as well as read the current traffic list. This information is broadcast simultaneously on all channels the company is authorized to use, giving you a perfect opportunity to surf channels until you find the strongest, clearest signal. If you can hear them well, they can hear you well.

Some enterprising marine businesses maintain private coast stations that allow boaters to call, at no cost, for products and services. Often included in this category are marinas, yacht clubs, towing services and salvage companies, and sometimes a business owned by the skipper of a distant vessel.

A single sideband can also provide access to transmissions you might never have considered, such as commercial airline flights, the U.S. Air Force or Air Force 1 (the President's airplane), Interpol, the Hurricane Research

Electronics Aboard -- By Stephen Fishman

Center in Florida, the CIA, Antarctic stations and more. One of the more useful, if mundane, signals is the official worldwide consolidated time, broadcast as "tick, tick, tick, at the sound of the tone it will be exactly..."

Typical Features

Like vendors of other marine electronics, manufacturers of single sideband transceivers are constantly updating their radios with more controls, easier operation and expanded functions. Still, the specifications of many of these systems are similar, and nearly all systems include an automatic tuning antenna coupler (but no antenna). Most currently available single sideband radios offer these features:

- 150 watts of peak power
- User-programmable receive channel memory
- One-touch access to the international distress frequency 2,182 kHz
- Keypad command entry
- An alphanumeric display of each channel
- A large LCD display
- Variable squelch control
- A weather-resistant case
- Frequency scanning
- Two-tone SOLAS alarm
- Multiple mounting options, including tabletop, overhead or flush-mount
- Optional external speaker
- Optional Telex capability with an accessory terminal
- Optional remote stations

This may seem like a long list but it's important to bear in mind that the capabilities of an SSB are extensive and are increasing all the time. While a point-by-point comparison of the features offered by several manufacturers would be a valuable exercise for anyone contemplating a sideband purchase, I would like to make just three main points:

- The more power, the better. Some SSBs offer no more than 20 watts of peak power. If you are ever in trouble, you're probably out of luck with a unit like this.
- A large, bright LCD display is not only desirable but, in my view, necessary. You want to be able to easily see the display both during the day and at night, whether or not you're wearing your contact lenses.
- Single-button access to 2,182 kHz, the international distress frequency. If you need help, you need help now!

After these basics, go for whatever gadgets you feel the most comfortable with providing, of course, that your wallet can support it.

Figure 12-3

Sideband remote unit

Some private coast stations now offer voice mail services that, for all practical purposes, provide the same function as an answering machine on your telephone at home. Friends, family and marine businesses can leave messages for voyagers and, in return, travelers can leave messages for others to retrieve. Rumor has it that this service was the idea that developed into Call Notes® and other electronic message offerings from Southwestern Bell and other land line service providers.

Antennas

This is as critical a topic for single sideband as it is for any other type of transceiver, but an SSB has different requirements for powerboats and sailboats. While a marine VHF radio might use the same antenna for any type of vessel, there are very specific types of antenna for these two classes of boats.

For power craft smaller than about 16 feet in length, a 6-foot fiberglass whip antenna would probably work best because it requires no antenna tuner and won't overwhelm the vessel in cost or bulk. For larger powerboats, a 23-foot fiberglass antenna is recommended. The antenna connects to an automatic antenna tuner and provides almost instant readiness for use.

Caution! *Be certain to mount the antenna away from a tuna tower or a flybridge if it has an extensive enclosure. The metal frame will absorb a significant amount of the radio's transmit and receive energy, resulting in a major loss of signal strength.*

Sailboats, on the other hand, require a much different antenna arrangement. Most sailboat owners install an antenna for a single sideband on an insulated backstay attached to the existing metal backstay of the standing rigging. These antennas work extremely well and are preferred as much for their clean appearance as their efficient operation.

Beware, though, that should a dismasting occur you will have lost your antenna at the very moment you need it the most. As a result, every sailboat equipped with an insulated backstay antenna should also have a whip antenna as a backup. A spare antenna of this type is usually a 6-foot multi-band antenna mounted on the stern rail, similar to the type used on smaller vessels all the time.

As a side note, many antennas work and play well with others, which allows you to combine antennas on your boat in an effort to keep the superstructure of your vessel from looking like an antenna farm. Here are some common combinations of antenna use:

- Citizens band (CB) and marine VHF
- Marine VHF and Loran C
- Weather fax and Ham radio
- Ham radio and marine SSB
- Television and AM/FM stereo

Grounding

One of the unique things about a single sideband transceiver is the quality of the equipment matters far less than the quality of the installation. Both the radio and the antenna must be electrically bonded to a ground that is elaborate in design, but relatively straightforward to install.

As mentioned early in this chapter, an SSB signal is actually one of two mirror-image signals; the tandem signal is removed from the transmission along with the carrier wave. The purpose of the ground is to restore that mirror-image signal, called a counterpoise. Without this duplicate waveform, the antenna can't send out a single sideband signal.

It's like the FM dipole antenna you might have had attached to your stereo in your college days. I don't know about you, but the dorm I lived in when I was in college was the human equivalent of a densely populated hamster hotel. Everyone had a stereo of some kind and the reception was usually awful. A braniac friend of mine suggested I buy a dipole antenna and, sure enough, the reception was terrific.

Electronics Aboard -- By Stephen Fishman

The bare leads were connected to the antenna posts on the receiver, the wire ran vertically up the wall and then split in two directions like a big letter "T."

Well, the ground for a sideband transceiver works the same way. In this system, however, the groundplane installed in the boat is one half of the "T" while the other half is a fiberglass antenna.

In The Boat

The two components needed for a successful ground installation are copper foil and lots of connections to fittings below the waterline. It's critical to use foil as opposed to copper wire because even wire as thick as an inch in diameter tends to cancel out radio signals and, as a result, appears to be invisible as a counterpoise. If the foil is laid in when the boat is under construction, the task of creating the groundplane is incredibly simplified. Unfortunately, most boatbuilders feel the extra cost is unwarranted for the vast majority of their buyers. As a result, you'll have to install the groundplane the hard way.

Copper foil is available from many marine suppliers in rolls 3-inches wide. In a pinch, 1-inch plumbers foil tape would do but, if you can get it, use the larger size. The thickness of the foil is of no consequence, only the width. As you're making turns and bends, the foil can be bent on itself for 90-degree turns and can even be loosely rolled along its length if you have to pass through bulkheads, stringers and other structural members.

The most important aspect of the installation is to make sure you attach the foil to as many fittings as possible - through-hull valves, metal water or fuel tanks, the engine block and, the lead or iron keel in a sailboat. If your boat has a bonding system, follow the copper bonding wire and attach the foil to the same places.

In most vessels, it's a good idea to install a grounding plate on the exterior of the hull. For a powerboat, a plate could be attached to the transom, while a good location on a sailboat might be just aft of the keel near the centerline.

Don't forget the little stuff – stainless steel hose clamps, copper hydraulic steering lines, copper fuel or water lines, a wiper brush on the prop shaft - virtually anything metal below the waterline is a candidate for inclusion in the groundplane.

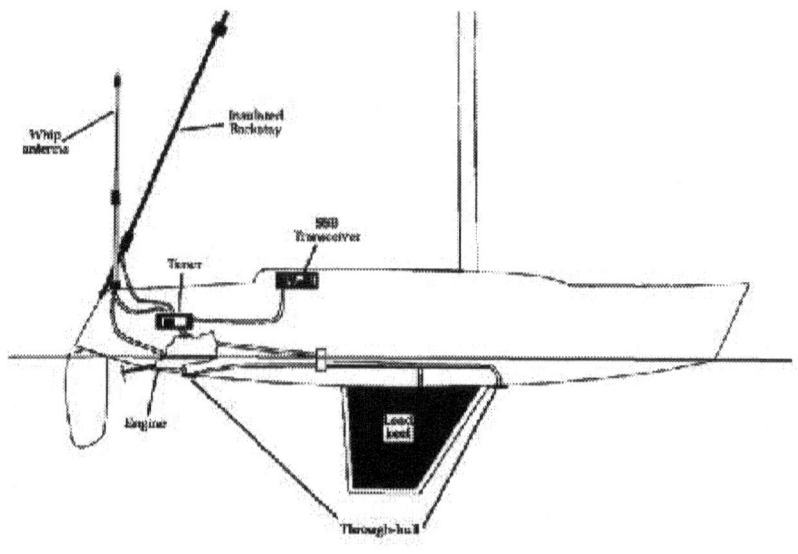

Figure 12-4

Creating a groundplane

Proper installation will require *no less* than a hundred feet of foil. As much of this as possible should be located below the waterline. Copper foil can be glued to the inside of the hull and painted, it can be left exposed and it can even be attached to the underside of lockers.

For sailboats, two points are worth mentioning. First, consider tapping a hole in the top of the keel where it meets the underside of the bilge. Attaching copper foil in this way instead of to a keelbolt is highly recommended. This avoids the task of loosening and rebedding a keelbolt. In my opinion, as long as the keel is firmly attached to the hull, it's best to leave the bolts alone and tap a small, new hole.

Second, don't forget the base of the mast or, for deck-stepped masts, the compression post. Tying the mast into the groundplane is a precaution against significant damage in the event of a lightning strike. If you really want to do a first-class job, tie in all through-deck bolts that anchor the standing rigging through chainplates, stem fittings and tangs. Lightning strikes are, at best, unpredictable, but you can go a long way towards protecting yourself and your vessel by providing the most direct path possible to ground.

Note: *A lightning strike aboard any vessel can be mitigated with a good ground. Aboard a sailboat, however, a strike has the potential to blow out through-hulls and fry every piece of electronics. This, as the result of radiating energy can spread among the stays and shrouds.*

Attachment

After the foil has been run everywhere possible below the waterline, it's time to make the final connections. Many manufacturers don't provide a convenient method of attaching the foil to the transceiver, but it's an easy task to remove a couple of sheet metal screws at the rear of the unit and attach the foil. If the vendor has provided a ground post, use it. In either instance, fold the end of the foil over itself two or three times before making the final connection.

Caution! *Under no circumstances should you use a jumper wire from the foil to the radio. Doing this will negate virtually all of your efforts at establishing a good groundplane.*

Copper foil can be easily drilled or soldered, which is good to know if you run a bit short of foil between the last connection belowdecks and the transceiver at the helm. Fold any extra foil back and forth several times, creating a sort of

Electronics Aboard -- By Stephen Fishman

accordion effect, so the radio can be easily removed should the need arise. While you're gounding, take a few moments to ground all of the instruments, using the same copper foil. The extra ground will eliminate most of the problems in the sideband signal caused by stray radio frequency noise produced by nearby instruments.

One precaution worth noting is the potential for damage to wiring from the sharp edges of the copper foil. Orient the foil so it is parallel to the wires coming into the rear of the instruments. If need be, either cover the edges of the foil with small-diameter vinyl tubing that's been split along its length, or cover the wires of the instruments with protective split vinyl tubing.

In addition to foil stretching from one end of the vessel to the other, there are two more ways you can enhance a groundplane. The first is with copper screens, similar to window screens for a house, that have been stretched across a frame. Copper screens are a mesh of fine copper strands surrounded by a flexible framework of somewhat thicker metal, all of which is combined into a rectangular shape of various dimensions. These screens can be glued to the inside of the hull or sandwiched between layers of fiberglass during the boat's construction. The screens can be fastened to the ceiling, the underside of lazarette or almost any location that provides a fairly flat, uninterrupted surface.

The second optional enhancement is to install additional foil as "radials" that extend the ground beyond the standard groundplane. Although not strictly necessary, foil radials can increase the effectiveness of a ground many fold, while adding little to the cost of the complete installation.

The foil must also be connected to the antenna tuner as well as the antenna. Think of these connections as if they were on opposite ends of a single cable, with the radio on one end, and the tuner and antenna on the other end.

Electronics Aboard -- By Stephen Fishman

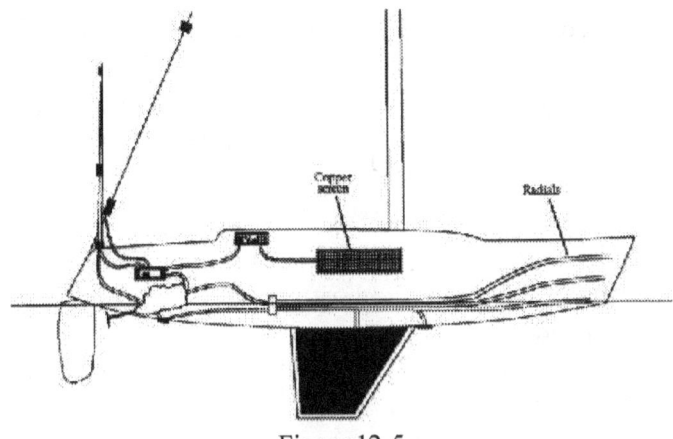

Figure 12-5

Copper screen and radials

The FCC Again

Now you have a good groundplane and the sideband transceiver, tuner and antenna have been installed, you're almost ready to go on the air. You may have accomplished the most perfect installation possible but, according to the Federal Communications Commission, you need to find someone else to agree with you. The FCC requires that a licensed technician sign off on your system in the ship's log and provide you with an FCC certificate.

As long as the technician is aboard, it's a good idea to have him (or her) check out and certify your equipment for proper installation and operation. Optimal radio operation is achieved when a technician checks out the antenna tuner, verifies that all connections are weatherproofed, makes radio signal field-strength tests and, in general, fine tunes your system. There is invariably a fee for this service but this is the very best way to guarantee you'll have the most efficient and trouble-free installation possible.

Don't forget to pick up a copy of the *Marine Radiotelephone User's Handbook* available for a modest

Electronics Aboard -- By Stephen Fishman

charge by contacting the Radio Technical Commission for Marine Services at RTCM, P.P. Box 19087, Washington, DC, 20036. This publication is a reference for FCC-approved methods of making and receiving calls on your single sideband.

Talking

Without question, the best way to begin using your new SSB is by listening to other people for several days, or more, to get the hang of how calls are made and become familiar with the general protocols. You should check out as many of the programmed channels as you can to get a feel for which frequencies are the strongest, and to gain a bit of experience estimating from what distance signals originate.

Your first call will most likely be for a radio check. Most commercial vessels will ignore your broadcast, but pleasure craft and idle marine telephone operators will almost certainly lend a hand. Remember, if the signal sounds weak when coming from another boat or a coast station then, in turn, your signal will sound weak to them. Don't panic. There is probably nothing wrong with your radio. You might want to try a different time of day, or move to the next band up or down. Keep in mind that the ionosphere is not a consistent, predictable reflective surface, so signal strength will continually be affected by conditions you can't control.

Check the high-frequency range of your radio by listening to foreign broadcasts or high seas transmissions. Typically, the signal will fade in and out in the higher bands at any given time, but this is normal and, once again, not a result of your radio installation.

If you plan to make ship-to-shore telephone calls with your sideband, you'll need to register with one or more of the four U.S. coast stations that provide high seas communications. This isn't necessary in order to access the service, but it is required if you expect them to bill you for the service in the same way that a land line telephone is billed.

Each coast station operates on eighteen channels, more

Electronics Aboard -- *By Stephen Fishman*

or less, so when you call they'll try to select a band that provides the strongest signal. To give them the opportunity to do this, you'll have to transmit for thirty seconds or so, repeating your ship's name and call letters along with the call letters of the station you're trying to reach. Coast stations are located primarily in the eastern portion of the United States at these addresses:

- Station WOO, AT&T, PO Box 558, Beach Avenue, Manahawkin, NJ 08050
- Station WOM, AT&T, 1350 NW 40th Avenue, Ft. Lauderdale, FL 33313
- Station WLO, Mobile Marine Radio, Inc., 7700 Rinla Avenue, Mobile, AL 36619
- Station KMI, AT&T, PO Box 8, Inverness, CA 94937

A single sideband transceiver is neither inexpensive to buy nor quick to install, but it can help provide a sense of community with other seagoing brethren, as well as a long-distance lifeline should an emergency arise.

Electronics Aboard -- By Stephen Fishman

Electronics Aboard -- By Stephen Fishman

Chapter Thirteen
Weather Fax

Of all the electronics available to mariners, perhaps the most overlooked aid to navigation is a weather facsimile. It's as easy to program as a VCR and relatively inexpensive. A weather fax allows you to receive and print satellite weather images that can help you avoid storms, find favorable breezes or arrange departure schedules based on weather conditions.

Available Data

With eighty locations in two-dozen countries around the world, weather fax signals are never far away. Broadcasts are generally every six hours from any given station, but each station has its own schedule.

Most weather faxes are fully tunable to any frequency between 2MHz and 23MHz, and weather information can be received through most. At night, you'll find 4MHz, 6MHZ, and 8MHz will be the strongest signals while, during the day, 12MHz, 16MHz and 22MHz will propagate better. Like single sideband signals, close proximity to a broadcasting station - 1,000 miles or less - will often require the use of a lower frequency for good reception.

The types of information available via weather fax include:

- Current general conditions
- A coastal marine forecast (up to fifty miles at sea)

Electronics Aboard -- By Stephen Fishman

- An offshore marine forecast (over fifty miles offshore)
- A surface analysis of wind and waves, along with air and water temperature data

All this information is presented in the form of satellite images enhanced with a variety of codes and symbols that can tell a skipper the area's current conditions.

Hardware

To receive weather fax broadcasts, you need a whip antenna, a high-frequency receiver such as a single sideband radio and a fax printer. If you don't have an SSB and don't want to invest in one, a receiver and printer in one unit may be your best choice, even though the investment will be marginally higher.

Unlike other antennas, the antenna for a weather fax can be installed belowdecks as well as out in the open. The only real caveat is that the antenna must have a substantial ground. The most convenient way of accomplishing this is to tie it in with the groundplane for a single sideband radio or a Loran receiver, if either is aboard. If not, a good RF ground similar to that needed for a single sideband must be established if you expect to receive weather transmissions on SSB frequencies. The construction of a groundplane is discussed in *Chapter 12: Single Sideband Radios.*

If you have a notebook computer aboard, you might want to consider a weather fax that can connect to your computer via an RS-232 serial port. If you have a modem in your computer already, it's probably configured as COM1; the weather fax should be configured as COM2. For more information about selecting communication ports, check the user manual that came with your computer.

It seems everyone has an opinion about the best radio or the best antenna, and weather fax is no different. Some skippers believe everything possible should be tied into an on-board computer – charting software, data displays, GPS and

Electronics Aboard -- By Stephen Fishman

even a weather fax. From the perspective of available real estate in the cabin or at the helm, this view may be the best idea for your vessel. For the most part, I agree, but there's a lot to be said for not putting all of your eggs in one computer. If you have a thick wallet, I would heartily recommend that you invest in a standalone weather fax receiver/printer and just deal with the issue of where to put it.

Figure 13-1

Furuno weatherfax

    As mentioned above, currently available weather facsimiles are fully synthesized and tunable. Except for loading paper, which in most cases can be either 8.5" or 11" wide, these devices operate on a sort of autopilot, coming alive only when a scheduled transmission occurs.

    In years past, weather fax used one of three types of paper, either illuminized, electrostatic or thermosensitive. Today, most weather faxes use the same type of paper as standard fax machines, either thermosensitive or plain paper. If you can afford it, a plain paper weather fax would be the runaway favorite.

Electronics Aboard -- By Stephen Fishman

Reading A Weather Chart

Getting the most out of a weather fax depends almost entirely upon how practiced you are in reading weather charts. Courses are available for a nominal fee through organizations such as the U.S. Power Squadron and the National Oceanic and Atmospheric Agency (NOAA) Weather Service, but a lot of experience can be gained by studying local television weather broadcasts. Local weather broadcasters use symbols to help describe weather conditions in the area. These same symbols are found on weather facsimile transmissions, along with a few others not typically used on television.

Note: *Bristol Fashion Publications has a book available titled* Marine Weather Forecasting, *writing by Frank Brumbaugh, which explains this subject in great detail including all the symbols you will ever see.*

Developing an understanding of weather fax symbols is fairly easy to accomplish. Some of the more common symbols used on weather charts are shown below.

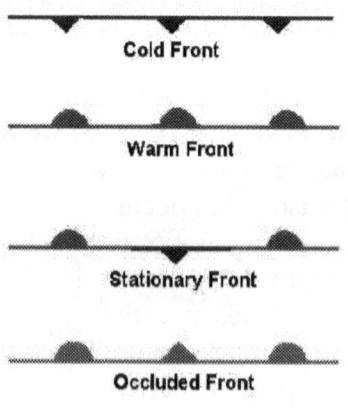

Figure 13-2

Common symbols of a weather chart

Electronics Aboard -- By Stephen Fishman

Fronts

A cold front is shown with triangles pointing in the direction the front is moving, with each triangle representing ten knots of wind speed. The direction of the wind is always clockwise at it passes through an area.

A warm front is shown on a chart by "blobs" that point in the direction of the front's movement and, like the triangles of a cold front, each blob represents ten knots of wind. The air in a warm front also moves clockwise as it passes through.

The symbols for a stationary front and an occluded front are similar. As its name implies, a stationary front is a band of weather that has ceased any significant forward movement across an area. A stationary front is shown with triangles and blobs on *opposite* sides of a single line.

An occluded front is a narrow zone of wind shift, and may be present in combination with another type of front. An occluded front is shown on a weather chart with both triangles and blobs on the *same* side of a weather line.

Clear skies are indicated with an open circle, while cloudy skies are depicted with a partly shaded circle. The amount of shading in the circle is an indication of how heavy the cloud cover is at the time of the broadcast, or how heavy it is predicted to be. Mostly cloudy skies are indicated with a completely shaded circle.

Other Conditions

Several letter abbreviations are used on weather maps in conjunction with specific symbols to designate different types of weather conditions. You may find many of the symbols fairly obvious representations:

F - fog   R – rain   T – thunder storms
Z – freezing rain   S – snow

Electronics Aboard -- By Stephen Fishman

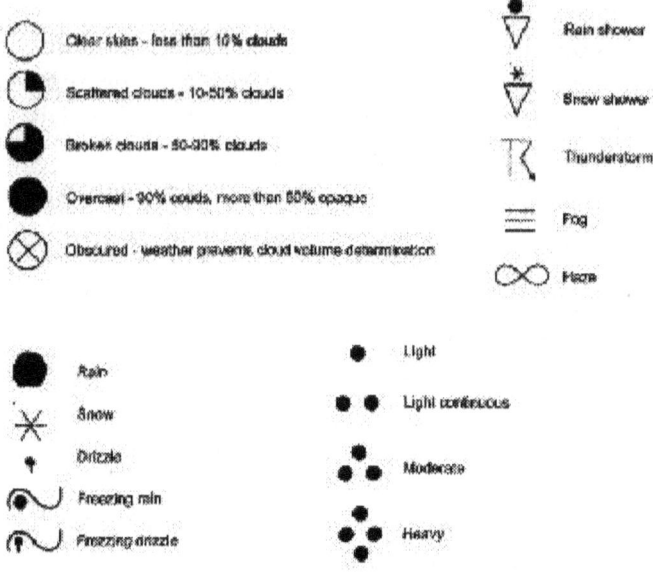

Figure 13-3

Common weather map symbols

Severe storms are not represented on weather charts, per se, but tropical storms are shown as an *open* circle with two curved "tails," and a hurricane is shown an a *shaded* circle with tails.

Yet another symbol common on weather charts is a group of symbols indicating wind direction and wind speed on the water. Learning this series of icons may take a bit more time than learning to recognize the presence of a cold front, but the information instantly learned from the data might be a lifesaver. The "flag" lines indicate the direction of the wind while the numbers indicate the range of wind speed; a pennant-shaped flag line is an immediate indicator of severe weather.

Electronics Aboard -- By Stephen Fishman

Wind Speed Code

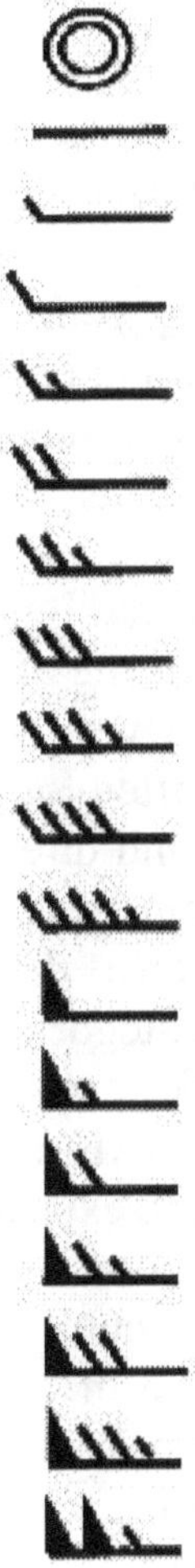

Symbol	Knots	MPH
⊚	Calm	Calm
—	1 - 2	1 - 2
⌐	3 - 7	3 - 8
⌐	8 - 12	9 - 14
⌐⌐	12 - 17	15 - 20
⌐⌐	18 - 22	21 - 25
⌐⌐⌐	23 - 27	26 - 31
⌐⌐⌐	28 - 32	32 - 37
⌐⌐⌐⌐	33 - 37	38 - 43
⌐⌐⌐⌐	38 - 42	44 - 48
⌐⌐⌐⌐⌐	43 - 47	50 - 54
▮	48 - 52	55 - 60
▮⌐	53 - 57	61 - 66
▮⌐	58 - 62	67 - 71
▮⌐⌐	63 - 67	72 - 77
▮⌐⌐	68 - 72	78 - 83
▮⌐⌐⌐	73 - 77	84 - 89
▮▮⌐	103 - 107	119 - 123

Figure 13-4

Wind speed and direction indicators

Electronics Aboard -- By Stephen Fishman

Using Weather Fax

A weather fax contains a tremendous amount of data, all of which is intended to keep you informed about weather conditions in your area. Every weather chart provides several types of information:

- A surface analysis, current conditions in your area
- A forecast of the weather to expect in your area during the next 24-36 hours
- A forecast of the weather along your route or at your destination during the next 24-36 hours
- A general forecast for large areas such as all of North America

Surface analysis charts primarily show current conditions, including highs and lows for the area, with updates every six hours. These updates predict weather conditions no more than 36-hours in the future, and often for a period of time as short as 18-hours. In addition to wind direction and speed, surface analysis charts show water temperatures as well as the course and speed of major currents, such as the Gulf Stream.

There are two general categories of weather information you must know and track to stay out of trouble while on the open sea. These are how existing major weather systems have developed and what they're expected to do.

It's good practice to make extra notes on a weather fax, indicating the location of anything that could seriously impact your safety. This includes the presence of any funnel clouds (water spouts), the type, position and movement of fronts, air temperature and precipitation predictions, and the positions of high and low atmospheric pressure areas.

Weather data should be monitored constantly, especially in deteriorating weather conditions or at times when the weather is changing quickly. At all times, it's the weather upwind that will have the greatest impact on your safety and comfort. If conditions are changing quickly or if the wind is

Electronics Aboard -- By Stephen Fishman

above ten knots, it's a good idea to check the weather as far away as 200 miles upwind. In slow changing conditions or wind speeds of less than about ten knots, look upwind 100 miles when reviewing forecast information.

In addition to air temperature and wind conditions, the appearance of waves is often an indicator of impending weather, with whitecaps the most familiar sign.

NAVTEX

Primarily found aboard commercial vessels and larger private yachts, NAVTEX – navigation telex – provides navigation and weather data up to about 400 miles offshore.

A NAVTEX unit is a standalone receiver that automatically receives signals at 518KHz, and displays the information on a built-in LCD screen. This is accomplished as it saves the data to memory. An audible alarm sounds when the incoming message carries severe weather data or other critical information, such as piracy or search and rescue efforts.

Many NAVTEX receivers have an integrated printer using three- to four-inch wide paper. Unlike a weather fax, a NAVTEX message doesn't include a map. Instead, the entire message is in text and it generally contains the entire contents of local and national weather forecasting.

Electronics Aboard -- *By Stephen Fishman*

Electronics Aboard -- By Stephen Fishman

Chapter Fourteen
The Wireless Option

There are devices that wake us up, cook our food and entertain us. There are gadgets that process words, keep track of our finances, transport us from one place to another and soothe us with wonderful music. In fact, the list of modern conveniences made possible by micro-miniaturization is almost endless. Of all these fabulous inventions, there is one device that is unique because it provides not only incredible communication capabilities but, at the same time, generates more animosity among its users (and nonusers) than any other device - the cellular telephone.

I can't count the number of times I've wanted to bash the skull of some idiot who refused to turn off his cell phone in a movie theater. Pagers are bad enough, but to have some inconsiderate, unthinking jerk talk on his phone as if he's sitting in his living room while I'm trying to enjoy a movie for which I paid dearly... but I digress.

For the most part, the reason given for wanting to get out on the water is to get away from phones, pagers, fax machines and all the other stuff that ties us to land and our daily routine. There's something incredibly freeing about being out of touch, even if it's only for an afternoon. When my wife and I set sail for the day, we leave behind as much of the real world as possible, including clocks and job-related machines. We make an honest attempt to get off the world for a while, knowing that the universe will get along just fine for a few hours without us.

Electronics Aboard -- By Stephen Fishman

That said, cell phones are everywhere, including aboard our boats. Regardless of how much I take issue with the darn things, when you stop to think about it, it makes sense. Personally, I don't own a cell phone but, on occasion, a guest will bring one aboard and we always seem to make good use of it. Sometimes we order a pizza for delivery to the dock with the intent that it will arrive when we do which, by the way, usually works out. Other times a phone is used to make reservations at one of the restaurants along the waterfront, or sometimes to just chat with other boaters.

All of which begs the question: Why aren't we using the marine VHF radio to do this stuff? The answer most often heard is "Why not?"

Indeed, Why Not?

Actually, there are at least five good reasons for using a cell phone on board instead of a VHF radio, especially when you're not far from land:

- There's no battle for air time
- Virtually every business and home has a telephone
- The range is often greater
- If a cell phone is on board, it's always turned on
- The big one - it's an exclusive, *private* call

Let's take a look at each issue in turn, beginning with #1, the battle for air time.

The FCC rescinded the requirement that all VHF radios had to be licensed to the vessel in which they were installed. When this occurred, the marine VHF mutated from a useful, boating-specific, communications device to the waterborne equivalent of a CB radio.

Now in decades past, I did a lot of traveling by car and, in the process, used the heck out of several CBs. I was never one those guys who sounded like he had a mouth full of marbles when he talked, but I did my share of yakking under

Electronics Aboard -- By Stephen Fishman

the "handle" of *Freelancer*. Unlike automobile-based CB radios, a marine VHF was, and still is, used more for real communication and less for nonsense. Unfortunately, a lot of people made the transition to from land-based transportation to watercraft but didn't leave the CB mentality in the garage.

If you've spent much time boating in popular coastal areas you're familiar with the problem. As a considerate skipper, you no doubt try to obey established protocol when using your VHF radio. Your reward is to be blown off the air or verbally trod upon by some dufus who doesn't care – or worse, doesn't know the rules. The result is it takes longer to accomplish the same task, and it's far more frustrating than it should be. Some of these idiots even go so far as to get upset with you for interrupting *them*!

The reality is that it's simply easier – and far less frustrating – to pick up a telephone and place a call, knowing you won't be interrupted or talked over. Of all the reasons for using a cell phone on a boat, this is the one that is given most often.

Every business and virtually every home has a telephone. While this is true, I long ago gave up trying to figure out why many marine-related businesses, as well as other businesses near the water, don't have and monitor a VHF radio. From my perspective, it seems obvious to even the casual observer that if you want boaters to communicate with your business, it's in your best interests to make it as convenient as possible for them to do that. What more convenient way could there be to call a marine supplier than with a marine radio? Maybe in the past, but given the proliferation of cellular phones, perhaps wireless communication is now a better option.

Unfortunately, there is no law that requires a pleasure boat to carry – let a lone use – a marine VHF radio. At the risk of insulting some people, most of us will choose the easiest path if we're presented with alternative methods of doing the same thing. For many, a cell phone is easier, if for no other reason than the fact that it's more familiar. Truth be told, we're

Electronics Aboard -- By Stephen Fishman

all creatures of habit and, as such, we will usually do what is most expedient, easiest, cheapest or the most familiar. To many boaters, a cell phone represents the answer to all four.

A cell phone gives new meaning to the term long-range, the actual distance being fundamentally a function of how far you are from shore. If you sail the Great Lakes – at least along the south and west shores - there is a preponderance of cellular and digital repeating towers. If you like to lose sight of land as soon as possible, however, your cellular phone will be of little use.

The range of a wireless phone is also a function of who's listening. Your phone is useless if no one's home, in the same way a marine VHF radio is useless if no one is monitoring channel 16. But it's far more likely *someone* can be reached by telephone than by radio.

If a wireless telephone is on board, it's almost guaranteed to be turned on, unlike a marine VHF radio which many weekend boaters don't switch on unless they have a need to use it. I have a real problem with this one because it makes me a little nervous to know there are, supposedly, responsible skippers out there who wouldn't know they were needed if something serious occurred.

I've lost count of the times I've been out on someone's boat and they refuse to turn on the VHF radio unless they intended to use it. When asked about why, they usually say because it's noisy and a nuisance, never giving a thought to the reason it was installed. It might be a nuisance to some, but only until it's *you* who needs it.

Only commercial vessels are required to monitor channel 16 but, over the years, I've been in a position to render aid or assistance on many occasions. In every instance, save one, the call for help came across the marine band and not the Bell band. Perhaps these same people would have used a cell phone if they'd had one, but perhaps not.

A telephone call is more likely to find an answer on land, but a marine broadcast is far more likely to find an answering voice in the immediate vicinity. However, this one can be argued either way.

The last often-heard reason given for favoring a cell phone over a marine radio is inarguable. It's a private call.

Actually, this isn't completely true. Anyone with the proper equipment can record any call made on any wireless telephone, and without spending a fortune. In practice, thankfully, this is rare since most of us aren't saying much worth recording. When compared to the casual eavesdropping capabilities of a marine VHF radio transmission, a cell phone call can be likened to talking to someone inside a vault. No one knows what you're saying and no one can interrupt you.

It's worth restating something that was stressed in *Chapter 4: VHF Radios* - there is no privacy when using a VHF radio. NONE! Interestingly enough, not everyone who uses a marine VHF radio knows this or, if they do, they don't much care who's listening. I've heard some wonderfully risqué conversations that were anything but private. You have to wonder what the participants are thinking. The only technology you need to be able to eavesdrop on a marine VHF radio broadcast is any marine VHF radio. If you ever considered the possibility of having a covert conversation on a marine radio band – forget it!

Rules & Regs

There no legal prohibitions, and I rather like it that way. Never mind the issue of government intervention in our lives, the truth for me is simply this: Anything you can bring aboard that will help assure your safe return is a good thing. Very little will do more for your safety than good communications, regardless of the device.

As it happens, the U.S. Coast Guard agrees, and so does every other law enforcement agency. They all take the position that if bringing a cellular phone aboard makes their job easier and the boating public safer, there's no reason to discourage it. One marine officer I talked to said he views this issue as an extension of the concept of system redundancy,

Electronics Aboard -- By Stephen Fishman

and welcomes every boater to be so conscientious.

What it comes down to is expediency. If a wireless telephone gets you help when you need it, then use it. If a phone is the most convenient method of dealing with the local gas dock, then call them.

Do yourself and your guests a favor by also installing and learning how to use a marine VHF radio. Monitor channel 16 for the benefit of others who might one day need your help. After all, I don't have a cellular telephone and I may want to chat with you using my VHF.

Extended Range

Like a marine VHF broadcast, wireless telephone transmissions can "bounce" off the underside of the ionosphere and reach antennas several hundred miles away. This occurs most often on hot windless days when warm air is trapped in an inversion layer beneath a high-pressure weather system. This condition, called tropospheric ducting, extends the reach of your phone from 15 miles or so to as much as 300 miles offshore. In the southern portion of the United States this condition can occur fairly regularly from mid-June through the end of August. The clear, long-range reception can continue for several days, or until the weather changes.

You certainly can't depend on an extended telephone broadcast range to be available when you really need it, but it does occur often enough to be aware of the possibility.

Marine cellular antennas can go a long way towards increasing the range of a wireless phone. Usually eight feet long and easily mounted near other antennas, a cellular antenna can eliminate the roaming charges still associated with some cellular contracts. We're not talking about a special telephone, either. It's not unusual to achieve a distance of fifty miles or more, which can keep you in touch with family and friends while you're still out of sight of land.

Electronics Aboard -- By Stephen Fishman

Alternatives

There are currently two noteworthy alternatives to cellular and PCS telephone service – Iridium and Globalstar satellite telephones.

Iridium, LLC's claim to fame is its satellite-to-satellite relay of voice and data. With a constellation of 66 low-earth orbit (LEO) satellites, Iridium can connect two of its handheld phones from anywhere on the globe.

Figure 14-1

Satellite telephone

The basic package includes two handheld phones and a docking station, which offers hands-free operation and a speakerphone. The handsets are larger and a bit heftier than typical cellular telephones, weighting in at about one pound each and six- to seven-inches in length. They are also more costly - $1,000 to $1,500, depending on the model, but considering what they can do that's not a bad price.

Iridium phone calls are handled either by using two Iridium handsets or by accessing standard terrestrial telephone lines. When you place a call using an Iridium phone, the call is picked up by the nearest satellite. After verifying the account,

Electronics Aboard -- By Stephen Fishman

the call is relayed to other satellites in the Iridium constellation until it reaches another handset or is connected to a public switched telephone network (PSTN). If the call is made between handsets, the cost is about a buck a minute, but if the call is made by connecting to a PSTN, the cost is about $1.50 a minute.

The future of Iridium phones looks pretty good - now. For several years, the company appeared to be headed the way of the dodo bird, but in recent years it has been purchased and revitalized, and is now a viable communications option. The company has contracted with Boeing for the operation and maintenance of its constellation (including seven spare satellites) as well as its control stations, and with Motorola for maintenance of the equipment purchased by subscribers.

In addition to voice, the system currently supports 2.4K baud data transmissions, with short burst messaging and 10K BPS enhancements scheduled for late 2001. The service is available through independent providers, who buy blocks of time and resell it to subscribers. Iridium's current resellers are mainly overseas companies.

Because all of the complex hardware is located on board the orbiting satellites, maintaining and upgrading their system offers significant challenges.

Globalstar completed its own constellation of 52 low-earth orbiting satellites in early 2000. Like Iridium, Globalstar calls are transmitted from proprietary wireless telephones and can be passed on to existing FSTN and cellular telephone networks. Unlike Iridium, however, Globalstar focuses on using "gateways" and working with terrestrial networks as opposed to isolating their network from other providers.

Electronics Aboard -- By Stephen Fishman

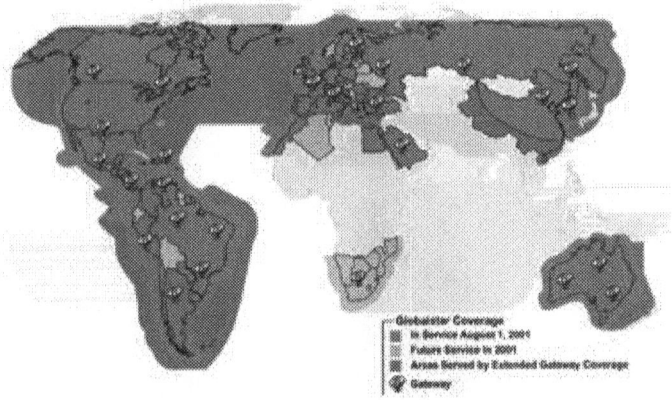

Figure 14-2

Globalstar coverage map

Because of this, their multimode phone is designed to operate on a cellular network when one is available, or on the Globalstar network when you're beyond cellular coverage.

In addition to voice calls, Globalstar offers services such as global roaming, fax and other data options, as well as short message burst capabilities.

Each gateway receives transmissions from orbiting satellites, then processes the calls and switches them to the appropriate ground network. Gateways consist of three or four dish antennas, a switching station and remote operating controls. Because all of the switches and complex hardware are located on the ground, it's easier to maintain and upgrade the system than if everything was in orbit.

Globalstar phones are supplied by several different manufacturers, including Ericson and QualComm, but they share many features:

Electronics Aboard -- By Stephen Fishman

Figure 14-3

Globalstar cellular/satellite phone

- Multiline graphical display
- A lithium-ion battery power source
- A clock with an alarm
- A fairly large LCD display
- Dual-mode GSM 900/Globalstar and automatic mode selection on power-up
- Programmable security levels
- Caller ID and call barring
- Call forwarding, call waiting and "hold"
- Short Message Service (SMS), which means that you can send and receive SMS messages in all modes

The cost for Globalstar satellite telephone service is about the same as Iridium when using PSTN lines, about $1.50 per minute.

So far, neither system appears to be emerging as the clear winner but, for my money, Globalstar probably has the edge.

Electronics Aboard -- *By Stephen Fishman*

The Connected World

Although this may be overwhelming technology for ordering a pizza, making a dinner reservation or calling about fuel prices at the local gas dock, it can be very useful in business. Granted, I go to the water to get away from it all, but not all boaters can leave it all behind when they go.

The technology of cellular and satellite phones make it possible for many people to cruise the waterways, even on extended voyages, while staying in touch with the office and clients. This is not limited to voice communications. The full array of fax, phone, E-mail, Internet and even credit card processing is still a phone call away while aboard. If you can do it in your office with a land line, you can do it onboard, although much slower.

The best system is a digital/analog cellular phone on the AT&T One Rate Plan. AT&T has the widest coverage area with virtually no roaming nationwide. One Rate means you pay the same rate (currently $.10 per minute) for local calls as for long distance calls. Although satellite phones will do the job, their slower connection speeds of 2.4K (5 to 6 minutes to send a one page fax) and high per minute cost makes it a prohibitive option for most.

Yes, you also need a computer. This can be a laptop or an office machine. If your laptop has a cellular ready modem and the cord to attach it to your phone you are ready to work aboard. If not, you will need both the cord and the PCMCIA cellular ready modem. Currently these two components cost about $160.00 with the prices dropping regularly.

If you would rather move your desktop PC on board than empty your wallet for a new laptop, it too can be setup to do the job. Of course, you lose the excuse to upgrade to a new computer.

To setup your desktop, you will need the cord, PCMCIA modem and one additional piece of equipment called a PCMCIA card reader. The card reader will mount in the back or front of the computer (the choice is yours) and connect to a

Electronics Aboard -- By Stephen Fishman

ISA or PCI slot on the mother board. Many now run through a USB hub. It is a very simple installation for all methods but be certain which type slot you have open BEFORE you order the card reader.

When the card reader is installed, simply slide the PCMCIA modem card in to the reader, plug the cord into the card and into the phone. The setup directions are included and easy to follow since the setup is very easy.

When all is complete, the connected world is at your finger tips but at a rate of no more than 9.6K (9600 bps). This equates to a VERY slow speed connection (1993 modem speeds). It is not meant to surf the web searching for the best price on one of my books. It's just too slow for the graphic intensive, high security web sites of today. It is meant to, and works very well to keep in touch with the day to day business world.

Electronics Aboard -- By *Stephen Fishman*

Chapter Fifteen
Installation Issues

Okay, let's dream a little. Let's say you're one of those truly blessed skippers who can afford to buy whatever electronics you want. You study the market (with the help of this book, of course) and you assemble all the components necessary for a really kickin' navigation system. You've picked out the perfect DGPS/chartplotter – with WAAS, naturally – along with an autopilot, speed and depth gauges, an incredible 15-inch LCD backlit display, a powerful single sideband radio and a marine VHF for close-in communications. Terrific!

But wait. Are you going to do the installation? Do you know about the little things that can mean the difference between a solid, reliable system and one that will desert you when you need it most? Have you ever seen wiring that looks perfect on the outside when there's nothing on the inside but air? Have you ever picked up a radio microphone and received a light electrical shock? Can you imagine where you might end up if your Loran isn't shielded from the fluorescent light in your galley?

All of these problems and many, many more can cause you untold hours of grief and many dollars in service calls if the equipment you install isn't wired correctly. Even if a marine electrical contractor does the work, every responsible skipper should know at least a little about the wiring aboard the vessel. After all, it's not like a car that you get out of and walk away. You never know if – or when - you might have to stand on your head in a lazarette and make a repair in the worst of conditions.

Electronics Aboard -- By Stephen Fishman

Wiring

In today's boats, all but the smallest of cruisers have two distinct and separate wiring systems – a 110-volt AC system similar to what we have in our homes and offices, and a 12-volt DC system that is akin to what we have in our cars.

Aboard a boat, 110-volts is needed for such things as air conditioning, hot water heater and a host of small appliances. For most of us, this means when we leave the slip behind we also leave behind the power that drives these devices. Fortunately, this is not the case with marine electronics.

Virtually all noncommercial marine navigation equipment operates on 12-volt DC current drawn from the ship's batteries. This wiring system is completely different - and significantly less hazardous - than a 110-volt system. It can be run in wet areas unthinkable for 110-volt AC wiring. Looking at the difference in the numbers says a great deal about the differences between the two systems. AC current carries nearly ten times the amount of voltage as DC current.

12-Volt DC Basics

The Wire

A 12-volt DC electrical system is a fundamentally simple concept. Every connected device has only two wires attached to it. The wires are insulated and generally color-coded – red for positive or "power" and black for negative or "ground." That said, DC wiring standards don't always hold true. Although positive is usually red and negative is generally black, positive also could be almost any color that has been coded for a purpose, while a negative wire could even be white. When 2-conductor wire uses both black and white, white is the positive and black is the negative lead. The color of the insulation is of no consequence; the main thing is to establish a color-coding standard aboard your boat and then keep it consistent throughout the vessel.

All wiring must be made from stranded copper wire as opposed to solid wire. Wiring made with a solid core is more susceptible to breakage as a result of vibration, but wire that is too finely stranded is likely to suffer corrosion problems so it, too, should be avoided.

The insulation of all wiring – both DC and AC – should be flame-retardant as well as moisture and oil-resistant. If not, the wiring must run through a fire-retardant material such as PVC pipe or some other protective sheath for the full length of the wire. This is especially true in wet areas such as the bilge and engine compartment. It's a good idea to inspect wiring insulation regularly for frays, cracks or excessive discoloration, and replace it as needed.

All wiring should be an appropriate gauge for the current draw, but 16-gauge should be considered the minimum size. Given the constant movement aboard a boat, small wires can be easily broken. Bear in mind that a long wire run from the battery to a device requires a heavier gauge wire than a short wire run. This hold true for a high current draw as well. Except for battery cables, 14-gauge and 12-gauge wire should be your standard sizes, depending on the device. See Figure 15-1.

To see a good example of this principle in action, raise the hood of your car and look at the size of various wires in the engine compartment. Spark plug wires are fairly thick, while wires coming from the alternator are a much smaller gauge. The largest wires are always the red and black primary battery cables, since these cables supply current to everything else.

Electronics Aboard -- By Stephen Fishman

WIRE USE CHART
3% VOLTAGE DROP, 12VDC WIRING

AMPS	LENGTH OF CONDUCTOR, SOURCE TO DEVICE & BACK TO SOURCE										
	10	15	20	25	30	40	50	60	70	80	100
5	16	16	14	12	12	10	10	10	8	8	6
10	14	12	10	10	10	8	6	6	6	6	4
15	12	10	10	8	8	6	6	6	4	4	2
20	10	10	8	6	6	6	4	4	2	2	2
25	10	8	6	6	6	4	4	2	2	2	1
30	10	8	6	6	4	4	2	2	1	1	0
40	8	6	6	4	4	2	2	1	0	0	2/0
50	6	6	4	4	2	2	1	0	2/0	2/0	3/0
60	6	4	4	2	2	1	0	2/0	3/0	3/0	4/0
70	6	4	2	2	1	0	2/0	3/0	3/0	4/0	
80	6	4	2	2	1	2/0	3/0	3/0	4/0	4/0	

Figure 15-1

Chart of wire size for amperage draw and length of run

The Route

Wires should be routed as high above the bilge as possible given the practical considerations of settees, stringers and other structural members. Do your best to avoid kinking or sharply bending wiring since this promotes metal fatigue,

Electronics Aboard -- By Stephen Fishman

eventually causing a fracture and conductor failure.

Support all wiring at intervals of no more than 18" unless they're run in the bottom of a conduit or trough. Screw down the supporting clips and, most especially, don't use nails or wire staples. It's important that none of the wiring move or flex with the boat. Make every effort to dampen vibrations from the engine or generator.

If wiring is run in a conduit or through a trough, even if it's high off the cabin sole, it's good practice to make drain holes to prevent water from collecting inside the conduit. This is especially true if you use your boat in the winter when the difference in temperature between a warm, cozy cabin and a cold hull causes condensation to collect on all interior surfaces.

Caution! *Under no circumstances should water be allowed to run along wiring to connections, fasteners or devices.*

Take care to protect wiring from damage in exposed areas where equipment is actively used, and from gear stored in lockers and lazarettes. In addition to direct contact with equipment, wiring must also be protected from chafing where it passes through bulkheads, junction boxes, and lockers.

All wires should enter terminals and equipment from below the location of the connector so condensation and other sources of moisture can be routed away from terminals. Creating a series of "drip loops" addresses this issue and, at the same time, results in an attractive installation that can be easily repaired.

Configuring each connection with a drip loop means you'll use a little extra wire on each run, but you'll also have enough wire to trim the end and attach a new connector should the need arise.

Electronics Aboard -- By Stephen Fishman

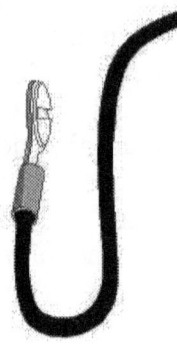

Figure 15-2

Drip loop wiring

Current Leak Test

A 12-volt DC electrical system should leak less than 5mA (milliamps) of current. You can conduct a simple test for DC current leakage by performing these steps:

- Turn off all DC circuits
- Rotate the battery switch to the OFF position
- Open the AC-DC panel
- Connect a sensitive digital ammeter (voltmeter) across the battery switch contacts or touch the contacts with the wires from an LED indicator light

Since you're looking for a solid indication regarding the presence (or not) of a leak above 5mA, either of the following results will tell you what you need to know.

- If an LED is used, the light will glow if more than 5mA is present across the contacts

- If an ammeter is used, the needle will indicate the amount of current leaking across the contacts

- Bilge pumps and float switches are a common trouble spot since they sit in water much of the time, so check this circuit in addition to the main battery switch

Grounding

The ground wires (the black wires) from the batteries, the engine, the negative bus bar, the bonding system, the generator (if you have one), the underwater ground plate (you'd better have one!), and the vessel's 110-volt safety-ground (you'd better have one of these, too!) must all meet at one point. If you have a fixed-mount LORAN receiver, the signal ground wire should also be connected to this common point. The common point must be a heavy bus bar or bracket with bolted connections.

This single connection location should be clearly labeled as the *Common Ground Point*; but we'll talk more about that later.

When reading an installation guide for 12-volt DC devices or when tracing down a problem by following a 12-volt DC wiring diagram, the text may alternately refer to a "ground," a "negative" wire, or a "ground return," all of which are equivalent terms.

Like all wiring, the DC ground needs to be easy to access and located as far above the bilge as practical.

One last point about grounds. The hull or bonding system ***must not be used*** for the ground. If you take this shortcut, you are likely to see accelerated corrosion problems in many areas on board.

Splices

Without question, any wiring run will be more secure and trouble-free far longer if it's made with a pair of wires absent of splices. Since this isn't always possible, do your very best to keep splices to a minimum with no more than one in any single run. Making a good splice is somewhat of an art and, almost without exception, a splice will end up in the most inaccessible place possible.

When a splice is unavoidable, it's best to take the time to solder the wires together and seal them from moisture with heat shrink tubing or electrical tape. Use a silver solder with a 60/40 resin core, and take care never to use solder with an acid core.

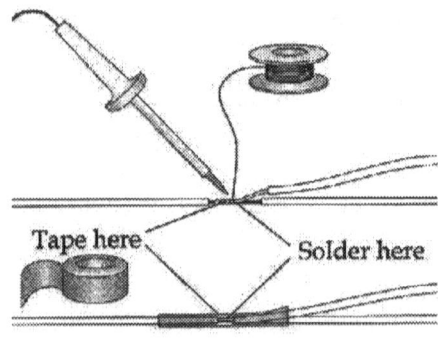

Figure 15-3

Solder splices

Connections held by solder alone will often fracture under even a small amount of stress. To help guard against this, wrap one wire around the other in a spiral before applying the solder. For maximum protection, coat the wires with clear nail polish after soldering and let the polish dry thoroughly before covering the splice. Other methods of joining wires before soldering include crimping them with a crimping tool or bolting them together.

Note: *Bolting two or more wires together prior to soldering works best when the joint is fastened to a solid surface of wood, metal or fiberglass.*

If you insist on making mechanical splices, strip back the insulation until you're sure there is enough wire to make a solid connection. Tin the wire by applying solder to the ends of the wires, and choose the correct size butt connector for the gauge wire you're using. Wire strands that are smashed inside a connector are extremely susceptible to vibration breakage. Take care to apply pressure only to the bare portion of the wire and not to the insulation. Some commercially crimped splices may work well without soldering but even these are fallible in a marine environment.

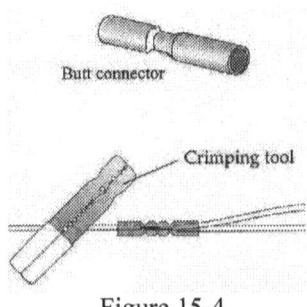

Figure 15-4

Mechanical butt splice

Under no circumstances should you ever make a connection by using wire nuts or wire screws by themselves. This technique may work well at home where nothing moves, but it can be disastrous on a boat. A quick fix of this type leaves bare wires exposed to the elements and, even if this weren't the case, there is nothing to prevent the wire nut from coming loose.

As a general rule, electrical tape doesn't hold up well in a marine environment and is a poor alternative to heat shrink tubing. That said, if tape is used for moisture protection on a splice or to insulate an awkwardly shaped connection, secure the finished end with a nylon wire tie or cover the end of the tape with heat shrink tubing to keep the tape from unraveling.

In places where wire vibration or movement is unavoidable, and especially in areas where wires are hidden from view, leave a little extra wire in loose coils at several intervals. By doing so, the movement of any given section of wire is minimized, and there is little chance that the wire will be pulled tight. Loose coils will also provide you with extra wire in several places, negating the need to make a new run should a break occur.

Connections

Mechanical connections can be quite strong if they include either a self-tapping screw in metal, a machine screw fastened into a tapped metal hole, or a machine screw with a washer and nut. Self-tapping screws fastened to wood, or to a thin wall of fiberglass or sheet metal, do not provide a reliable long-term mechanical connection that can withstand vibration and shock.

In all cases, the contact surfaces of mechanical connections need to be as clean as possible and coated with a moisture-resisting film, such as Corrosion Block™, before being joined together. "Star" type lock washers are best for bolted and screwed connections because they dig into the metal surfaces, providing an excellent metal-to-metal contact. This method of making mechanical connections by using a combination of a moisture-blocking spray and lock washers creates a sort of "locked" connection that will last indefinitely.

All wires should be anchored close to connections for strain relief and, as discussed earlier, it's best to make a drip loop.

Whenever possible – which should be virtually all the time – use ring terminal connectors of an appropriate size for the final connection to any device or to a terminal strip. Avoid spade or other types of "push on, pull off" connectors.

Ring connectors hold best if a wire is accidentally pulled or if a connection loosens. If spade connectors must be used, make sure they're clean, coated with a corrosion preventative, and positioned so water can't collect in the connection. In addition, create a strain relief by anchoring the wire with a drip loop in the same way as described for a ring terminal connector.

Electronics Aboard -- By Stephen Fishman

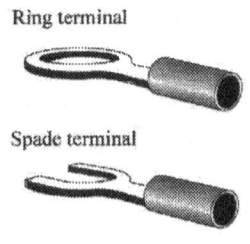

Figure 15-5

Ring and spade terminals

A better option is to install a terminal strip to which you can make ring terminal connections, and then seal the entire terminal strip. Terminal strips are much easier to clean than multiple terminal connections on several devices and all the connections can be covered with a single enclosure. The minimum size fastener for most terminal strips is a #8, and this is most commonly a #8-24 by one half-inch machine screw. Smaller fastener sizes often result in stripped threads and are rarely used.

All connections at a voltage different from the common ground – which includes all positive (red) wires in a 12-volt DC system - are usually insulated with shrink tubing or rubber boots at the connection point. In addition, most red wires carry an in-line fuse or circuit breaker to help protect the connected device against a short or a voltage spike.

It's a good idea to cover all connections - especially connections in an exposed area such as a flybridge or cockpit – with petroleum jelly, a water-resistant grease, or silicone. In addition, most marine electricians also seal the base of light bulbs, replaceable fuses and other friction connections. Move the connection back and forth a few times to create good metal-to-metal contact while squeezing the sealant aside. Applying sealant only to the exterior of connections might help prevent deterioration but it will be short-lived. Sealing the interior surfaces before assembly creates a much longer-lasting moisture barrier.

Electronics Aboard -- By Stephen Fishman

Labels & Schematics

Creating a schematic of your vessel's electrical systems can save you more aggravation than anything else when it's time to track down a problem. Of all the recommendations about the installation and maintenance of marine electrical systems, this is the one people are the least likely to follow.

Drawing a diagram of your boat's 12-volt DC electrical system – and another for the 110-volt AC system – isn't difficult. It does, however, require that three critical conditions be present. You have to want to make the effort. You have to devote the time to it. You have to plan for it by making copious notes as you install equipment and make repairs. From personal experience, I can tell you, the first is unusual, the second is unlikely and the third is unheard of.

Nonetheless, if you're willing to set aside the time and make the effort to create an electrical schematic, you will have one of the greatest timesaving devices of the modern world.

In case you haven't figured it out by now, I think this is a GREAT idea.

The planning required to make a schematic is simple to say but tedious to do. My suggestions follow.

Label every wire - at both ends. The label can't be too cryptic. The description should easily determine what the device is and where the wire is likely to lead.

The wiring should, ideally, be color-coded, either by purpose, by area or by subsystem. For example, you could install all cabin lights with blue positive wires and all cabin fans with green positive wires, creating two groups by purpose. Alternatively, all cabin wiring could be blue and black, while all masthead wiring is green and black, establishing a coding system by area.

An example of subsystem color-coding is to use a unique color combination for all ship's instruments – wind, depth, speed, temperature - and a different color scheme for all piloting equipment – autopilot, GPS, radar, chartplotter, etc.

The same gauge of wire should be used for all devices

Electronics Aboard -- By Stephen Fishman

within a group. If the builder or the previous owner didn't consider this important, you may find yourself rewiring some or all of the vessel's equipment.

Every electrical subsystem should be documented with diagrams of one sort or another and need not be created by a professional. Ideally, schematics should indicate the color or number, the size (gauge) wire and the device to which it's connected.

If you're trying to create a schematic from existing wiring, you may find that wires have been painted or covered in fiberglass, thus hiding their color.

A wiring diagram is easier to follow if wires are numbered. Tags can be made from white electrical tape or white wire insulation that has a large enough inside diameter to slide over other wires. Mark the number or letter using an indelible marker such as a Sharpie® felt tip pen, and then cover the notes with clear heat-shrink tubing. Another solution is numbered wire labels, available at electrical supply houses. The labels come in a dispenser of ten different rolls numbered 0 to 9. The label is pulled from the dispenser and wrapped aroung the wire. These labels are used extensively in commercial wiring where thousands of wires must be labeled for connection into a building's electrical distribution panels.

An alternative to tape or insulation labels is to use small squares cut from a sheet of 1/16" or 1/8" plastic, available at most hobby stores. Drill a small hole in each square and attach it to the appropriate wire with a nylon zip tie.

Lastly, it's a good idea to collect all diagrams and schematics, product information sheets, operating manuals, etc. and store them in one location on board. For me, this has always been the same place I keep insurance, registration papers and other important documents.

Fuses, Breakers & Switches

Every circuit **MUST** be protected with a fuse or breaker.

Electronics Aboard -- By Stephen Fishman

LET ME REPEAT THAT!

Every circuit **MUST** be protected with a fuse or breaker. The exception might be the starter motor circuit, but even that's debatable.

In a 12-volt system, all fuses and breakers, as well as switches, are wired into the positive side of a circuit. Breaking the negative side of a circuit with a blown fuse can cause stray current corrosion. This is something you definitely don't want. When this type of corrosion begins, it accelerates its damage as time passes to a degree unmatched by any other type of corrosion. One of the reasons this type of corrosion is so pervasive is the water in which the vessel sits acts as a conductor, magnifying and spreading the effect.

All breakers except electric motor breakers should be a trip-free type so they can't be overridden. They should be rated for no more than the rating of the smallest wire they protect. Electric motor fuses or breakers should be rated for no more than 125% of the maximum load of the motor.

Ideally, there should be no automatic reset breakers on board, such as thermal cutout breakers, unless the circuit is also protected by a fuse or a breaker that can be manually reset.

All fuses or breakers should be located inside the primary power panel with the possible exception of the main fuse or breaker for the entire system. If a fuse or breaker can't be installed on a circuit inside the primary panel, it needs to be in the battery side of the circuit.

Avoid in-line fuses unless they're providing secondary protection for a device, or if they're meant to protect a device on a shared circuit. They must be easily accessible so changing a blown fuse is not a chore. The protected end of the fuse holder should be connected to the battery end of a positive wire. In a 12-volt system, the fuse or breaker protecting the primary positive battery lead to the power panel should be located as near as possible to the battery end of the wire.

In general, the contacts inside of fuses should be clean,

tight, and well sealed. This can be accomplished with electrical tape, heat shrink tubing or silicone sealant.

The wiring in the main power panel must be readily accessible for maintenance and well ventilated, especially in warm, humid climates like those of the southern states. The main power compartment and its junction boxes should be made of plastic or some other nonflammable material. Under no circumstances should junction boxes be made of metal. In recent years, PVC as well as other types of plastics have come into widespread use by boatbuilders as a means of keeping down costs while providing safer materials.

As with the color-coding on wiring, all switches should be labeled for the device they control. If the engine is powered by gasoline as opposed to diesel, switches in the engine compartment and the fuel tank storage area must be ignition-protected and approved for marine use.

Finally, switches in the head, cockpit and any other moist areas should have rubber or soft plastic covers for moisture protection.

Tools

One of the best things you can do for yourself is to assemble a tool bag with the greatest range of use while minimizing the storage space required. For me, this means a well-thought out canvas tool bag.

Tools are needed for three types of repairs - mechanical, electrical and plumbing. Mechanical repairs are tasks such as removing and rebedding stanchions or installing a new block. Electrical repairs might be repairing a cabin light or replacing a depth gauge. Plumbing repairs may include replacing fresh water lines, installing a head repair kit or maintaining through-hull valves.

As you might guess, most projects include elements of two or more repair categories, which is why it's essential that your tool bag be as diverse as possible. Although mechanical repairs are by far the largest category and certainly a necessary

Electronics Aboard -- By Stephen Fishman

part of any electronics installation, navigation instruments require a focus on tools for electrical problems.

You'll undoubtedly need an electrical extension cord for 110-volt AC tools. Purchase one or more insulated in a round casing as they're less prone to tangling. Be certain they're made with a minimum of 14-gauge wire – 12-gauge is better - and fitted with a three-prong grounded plug.

Caution! *Under no circumstances should you ever use a two-prong adapter with a three-prong 110-volt AC plug, especially while working on a boat. AC can easily mean Angels Calling.*

You'll need a few specialty tools, and chief among them is a crimping tool. This multipurpose tool can strip up to eight sizes of wire as well as crimp the three most common sizes crimp connectors. Unfortunately, a crimping tool leaves something to be desired when cutting wire, so a good set of wire nippers, or "dikes," or linesman pliers is indispensable. With difficulty, nippers can be used to strip the insulation from wire, but you'll usually lose a few strands of wire along with the insulation. It's best to use the wire stripping portion of the crimping tool. Taken together, these hand tools provide the best means of stripping and cutting almost any size wire or wire connector.

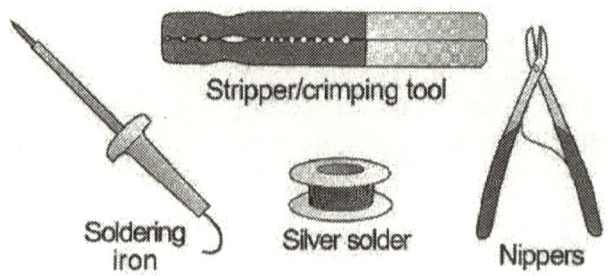

Figure 15-6

Common hand tools for electrical projects

Electronics Aboard -- By Stephen Fishman

Without question, you'll have to have a soldering iron or soldering gun. For delicate work, which includes almost all navigation electronics installations, a soldering iron is preferable to a gun unless the pistol is a low-voltage model. A soldering gun is often too hot for most uses and will often melt the insulation instead of merely heating the wire. A soldering iron works well with lower heat, it's smaller and lighter, and has a long tapered tip that gets into small spaces. With either type, be sure to use resin-core silver solder, as mentioned earlier, for long-lasting connections.

Add sharp scissors and a good pocketknife to your tool bag and your basic tool kit is complete. My choice for a pocketknife is a Swiss Army® knife model "Explorer®". It always seems to have just the right blade or accessory, including a corkscrew for the end of the day. Another good choice is a Leatherman or Gerber Tool. With all their accessories they can be a real "step saver".

There are several other tools you'll need to accomplish almost any equipment installation, including a drill, a measuring tape and screwdrivers, along with assorted fasteners. You might need a hole saw and you most likely will wear out several pair of needle-nose pliers. The particulars of your vessel and the types of materials you're working with will dictate the need for any other special tools.

Electronics Aboard -- *By Stephen Fishman*

Electronics Aboard -- By Stephen Fishman

Chapter Sixteen
Nothing Lasts Forever

The average life cycle of marine electronics is about the same as in any other area of our lives – five years. The question that begs to be answered is, "Where do all the old gadgets go?" The answer may not be what you expect.

In 1998, it was estimated that Europe had generated about six million tons of electronic waste. The expectation is to double that figure by the year 2010. It's safe to say that the United States isn't far behind.

This year, the European Parliament and the Council of Ministers are considering proposals that would reduce electronic waste, as well as increase recycling and reuse or recovery of electronic components. Regulations due to take effect by 2004 require manufacturers to build products that are more readily recycled, coded and identified for reclamation. An extension of this directive is the elimination of hazardous materials, such as lead and cadmium, by the year 2008.

In the U.S., the National Recycling Coalition estimates that in the ten years between 1997 and 2007, approximately 500 million personal computers will become obsolete. Most of these will be "dumped" in one way or another. The best guess is most of these PCs will find their way into landfills. Collectively, there will be millions of pounds of toxic substances threatening groundwater and wildlife. In addition to lead, cadmium, mercury and chromium can leach out of circuit boards, electrical switches and monitors.

Currently, there are three ways we can responsibly deal

Electronics Aboard -- By Stephen Fishman

with a PC that has reached the end of its useful life – refurbish it, donate it or recycle it. Although refurbishing a PC with a faster processor or larger hard drive is commonplace, most marine electronics don't lend themselves to component upgrades. As a result, the latter options make the most sense for communication and navigation equipment.

Donating older (but operable) single sideband, ham or VHF radios to the Sea Scouts, the U.S. Power Squadron and other maritime nonprofit organizations can put working equipment into the hands of less affluent or younger boaters.

If gear is in need of repair that outstrips the cost of replacement - which is growing more commonplace - marine electronics can usually be recycled at the same collection centers as a home PC. According to *Real Money*, a monthly newsletter published by Co-Op America, some of these centers are:

- Another BytE – www.recycles.org
- Electronics Industries Alliance Consumer Education Initiative – searchable Web database of donation centers and recyclers. www.eiae.org 703-907-7500
- National Cristina Foundation – www.cristina.org 800-274-7846
- Computer Recycling Center – whatever you've got, they'll accept. www.crc.org 408-317-1800

The marine industry will probably see a disposal fee collected at the retail level when an item is purchased. Local authorities will establish an appropriate amount and collection method.

One of the biggest problems facing manufacturers is products in development right now will be brought to market about the same time pending laws take effect. Unfortunately, this means they'll have to predict what the final regulations will demand and create their designs accordingly.

Electronics Aboard -- By Stephen Fishman

Appendix A
Navigation and Display Terminology

2D Mode
    A two-dimensional position fix that includes only horizontal coordinates. It requires a minimum of three visible satellites.

3D Mode
    A three-dimensional position fix that includes horizontal coordinates plus elevation. It requires a minimum of four visible satellites.

Acquisition Time
    The time it takes for a GPS receiver to acquire satellite signals and determine the initial position. Three satellites are needed for a 2D and four for a 3D-position fix.

Active Leg
    The segment of a route currently being traveled.

Almanac Data
    Information transmitted by each satellite on the orbits and state (health) of the entire constellation. Almanac data allows the GPS receiver to rapidly acquire satellites as soon as it is turned on.

Anti-Spoofing
    Encryption of the P-code to protect the P-signals from being "spoofed" through the transmission of false GPS signals by an adversary.

Electronics Aboard -- By *Stephen Fishman*

Atomic Clock
A very precise clock that operates using the elements Cesium or Rubidium. A Cesium clock has an error of one second per million years. GPS satellites contain multiple Cesium and Rubidium clocks.

Azimuth
The horizontal direction from one point on the earth to another measured clockwise in degrees (0-360) from a north or south reference line. An azimuth is also called a *bearing*.

Beacon
Stationary transmitter that emits signals in all directions, also called a non-directional beacon. In DGPS, the beacon transmitter broadcasts pseudorange correction data to nearby GPS receivers for greater accuracy.

Bearing
The compass direction from a position to a destination, measured to the nearest degree, also call an *azimuth*. In a GPS receiver, bearing usually refers to the direction to a waypoint.

Coarse Acquisition Code (C/A Code)
The standard positioning signal the GPS satellite transmits to the civilian user. It contains the information the GPS receiver uses to fix its position and time. Accurate to 100 meters.

Cold Start
The power-on sequence when the GPS receiver downloads almanac data before establishing a position fix. Also called *initialization*.

Control Segment
A worldwide chain of monitoring and control stations that control and manage the GPS satellite constellation.

Coordinate
A set of numbers that describes your location on or above the earth.

Coordinated Universal Time (UTC)
Replaced Greenwich Mean Time (GMT) as the World standard for time in 1986. It is based on atomic measurements rather than the earth's rotation. Greenwich Mean Time (GMT) is still the standard time zone for the Prime Meridian (Zero Longitude). It is the time kept by GPS satellites.

Course
The direction from the beginning landmark of a course to its destination (measured in degrees, radians, or mils).

Course Deviation Indicator (CDI)
A technique for displaying the amount and direction of crosstrack error (XTE).

Course Made Good (CMG)
The bearing from the 'active from' position (your starting point) to your present position.

Course Over Ground (COG)
Your direction of movement relative to a ground position.

Course To Steer
The heading you need to maintain in order to reach a destination.

Crosstrack Error (XTE/XTK)
The distance you are off the desired course in either direction.

Datum
A math model designed to fit part of the earths surface. Latitude and longitude lines on a paper map are referenced to a specific map datum. The map datum for a GPS receiver needs to match the datum listed on the corresponding paper map.

Desired Track (DTK)
The compass course between the "from" and "to" waypoints.

Differential GPS (DGPS)
A technique used to improve the accuracy of the GPS.

Electronics Aboard -- By Stephen Fishman

DGPS reduces the effect of selective availability, propagation delay, etc. and can improve position accuracy to greater than 10 meters.

Dilution of Precision (DOP)

A measure of the GPS receiver-satellite geometry. A low DOP value indicates higher accuracy. The DOP indicators are GDOP (geometric DOP), PDOP (position DOP), HDOP (horizontal DOP), VDOP (vertical DOP), and TDOP (Time clock offset).

DOD

The U.S. Department of Defense. The DOD manages and controls the Global Positioning System.

Elevation

The distance above or below average sea level.

Ephemeris

Current satellite position and timing information transmitted as part of the satellite data message. A set of ephemeris is valid for several hours.

Estimated Position Error (EPE)

A measurement of horizontal position error in feet or meters based upon a variety of factors including DOP and satellite signal quality.

Estimated Time Enroute (ETE)

The time left to your destination based upon your present speed and course.

Estimated Time of Arrival (ETA)

The time of day of your arrival at a destination.

Global Positioning System (GPS)

A global navigation system based on 24 satellites orbiting the earth at an altitude of 12,000 miles and providing very precise, worldwide positioning and navigation information 24 hours a day, in any weather. Also called the *NAVSTAR* system.

GLONASS

The Russian Global Positioning System.

GOTO

A route consisting of one leg with your present position

being the start of the route and a single defined waypoint as the destination.

Greenwich Mean Time
The mean solar time for the meridian at Greenwich, England, used as a basis for calculating time throughout most of the world. Also called *universal* time.

Grid
A pattern of regularly spaced horizontal and vertical lines forming square zones on a map used as a reference for establishing points.

Heading
The direction in which a ship or an aircraft is moving. This may differ from actual COG due to winds, sea conditions, etc.

I/O (Interface Option)
The one-way or two-way transfer of GPS information with another device, such as a nav plotter, autopilot, or another GPS unit.

Initialization
The first time a GPS receiver orients itself to its current location. After initialization has occurred, the receiver remembers its location and acquires a position more quickly because it doesn't need a large amount of satellite information.

Invert Route
To display and navigate a route from end to beginning for purposes of returning back to the route's starting point.

L1 Frequency
One of the two radio frequencies transmitted by the GPS satellites. This frequency carries the Coarse Acquisition Code, P-Code, and the nav message and is transmitted on a frequency of 1575.42 MHz.

L2 Frequency
One of the two radio frequencies transmitted by the GPS satellites. This frequency carries only the P-Code, and is transmitted on a frequency of 1227.6 MHz.

Electronics Aboard -- By Stephen Fishman

Latitude
    A position's distance north or south of the equator measured by degrees from 0 to 90. One minute of latitude equals one nautical mile.

Leg (route)
    A portion of a route consisting of a starting (from) waypoint and a destination (to) waypoint. A route that is comprised of waypoints A, B, C, and D would contain three legs. The route legs would be from A to B, from B to C, and from C to D.

Liquid Crystal Display (LCD)
    Produced by applying an electric field to liquid crystal molecules and arranging them to act as light filters.

Local Area Augmentation System (LAAS)
    The implementation of DGPS to support aircraft landings in a local area (20 mile range).

Longitude
    The distance east or west of the prime meridian (measured in degrees) which runs from the North to South Pole through Greenwich, England.

Long Range Radio Direction Finding System (LORAN)
    A radio navigation aid operated and maintained by the U.S. Coast Guard. It is used as a supplemental system for harbor approach navigation and inland navigation. LORAN C is used in civil aviation.

Magnetic North
    Represents the direction of the north magnetic pole from the observer's position. The direction a compass points.

Magnetic Variation
    Errors in magnetic compass readings caused by changes in the earth's magnetic field at different locations on the planet. Navigational charts list the variation and a yearly level of increase.

Map Display
    A graphic representation of a geographic area and the features in it.

Electronics Aboard -- By Stephen Fishman

Multiplexing Receiver

    A GPS receiver that switches at a very rapid rate between satellites being tracked. Typically, multiplexing receivers require more time for satellite acquisition, and are not as accurate as parallel channel receivers. Multiplexing receivers are also more prone to lose a satellite fix in dense woods than parallel channel GPS receivers.

Multipath

    An error caused when a satellite signal reaches the GPS receiver antenna by more than one path. Usually caused by one or more paths being bounced or reflected. The TV equivalent of multipath is "ghosting."

Nautical Mile

    A unit of length used in sea and air navigation, based on the length of one minute of arc of a great circle, especially an international and U.S. unit equal to 1,852 meters (about 6,076 feet).

Navigation

    The act of determining the course or heading of movement. This movement could be for a plane, ship, automobile, person on foot, or any other similar means.

Navigation Message

    The message transmitted by each GPS satellite containing system time, clock correction parameters, ionospheric delay model parameters, and the satellites ephemeris and health. The information is used to process GPS signals to give the user time, position, and velocity. Also known as the *data* message.

NAVSTAR

    The official U.S. Government name given to the GPS satellite system. NAVSTAR is an acronym for **NAV**igation **S**atellite **T**iming **A**nd **R**anging.

NMEA (National Marine Electronics Association)

    A U.S. standards committee that defines data message structure, contents, and protocols to allow the GPS receiver to communicate with other pieces of electronic

Electronics Aboard -- By Stephen Fishman

equipment aboard ships.

NMEA 0183

A standard data communication protocol used by GPS receivers and other types of navigation and marine electronics.

North-Up Display

A GPS receivers display screen always showing North on top.

Parallel Channel Receiver

A continuous tracking receiver using multiple receiver circuits to track satellites simultaneously.

P-Code

The precise code of the GPS signal typically used only by the U.S. military. It is encrypted and reset every seven days to prevent use from unauthorized persons.

Pixel

A single display element of an LCD screen. The more pixels, the higher the resolution and definition.

Position

A geographic location on the earth commonly measured in latitude and longitude.

Position Fix

The GPS receiver's computed position coordinates.

Position Format

The way in which the GPS receiver's position will be displayed on the screen. Commonly displayed as degrees and minutes, with options for degrees, minutes, and seconds, degrees only, or one of several grid formats.

Prime Meridian

The zero meridian ($0_¡$), used as a reference line from which longitude east and west is measured. It passes through Greenwich, England.

Pseudo-Random Code

The identifying signature signal transmitted by each GPS satellite and mirrored by the GPS receiver in order to separate and retrieve the signal from background

Electronics Aboard -- By *Stephen Fishman*

noise.

Pseudorange
The measured distance between the GPS receiver and the GPS satellite using uncorrected time comparisons from satellite transmitted code and the local receiver's reference code.

RS-232
A serial input/output standard that allows for compatibility between data communication equipment made by various manufacturers.

Radio Technical Commission for Maritime Services (RTCM)
A commission established for the purposes of establishing standards and guidance for interfacing between radiobeacon-based data links and GPS receivers, and to provide standards for ground-based differential GPS stations.

Route
A group of waypoints entered into the GPS receiver in the sequence you desire to navigate them.

Search the Sky
A message shown when a GPS receiver is gathering data from satellites to compute a position without almanac data.

Selective Availability (SA)
The random error which the government intentionally adds into GPS signals so that their accuracy, for civilian use, is degraded. The level of SA is subject to accuracy degradation to 100m.

Space Segment
The satellite portion of the complete GPS system.

Speed Over Ground (SOG)
The actual speed the GPS unit is moving over the ground. This may differ from airspeed or nautical speed due to such things as sea conditions or head winds. For example, a plane that is going 120 knots into a 10-knot head wind may have a SOG of 110 knots.

Electronics Aboard -- By *Stephen Fishman*

Statute Mile
A unit of length equal to 5,280 feet or 1,760 yards (1,609 meters) used in the U.S. and other English-speaking countries.

Straight Line Navigation
The act of going from one waypoint to another in the most direct line and with no turns.

TracBack
The GARMIN feature which takes your current track log and converts it into a route to guide you back to a starting position.

Track-Up Display
The direction to be followed, is always located at the top of the display.

Track (TRK)
Your current direction of travel relative to a ground position (same as COG).

Triangulation
The location of an unknown point, as in GPS navigation, found by using the laws of plane trigonometry.

True North
The direction of the North Pole from your current position. Magnetic compasses are slightly incorrect due to effects of the Earth's magnetic field. GPS units correct for magnetic influences.

Turn (TRN)
The degrees which must be added to or subtracted from the current heading to reach the course to the intended waypoint.

Universal Time Coordinated (UTC)
A universal time standard, referencing the time at Greenwich, England. Also referred to as GMT or Zulu time.

Universal Transverse Mercator (UTM)
A worldwide coordinate projection system utilizing north and east distance measurements from reference

Electronics Aboard -- By Stephen Fishman

point(s). UTM is the primary coordinate system used on U.S. Geological Survey topographic maps.

U.S.C.G
United States Coast Guard. The Coast Guard is responsible for providing all of the navigation aids in the U.S. including DGPS.

User Interface
The way in which information is exchanged between the GPS receiver and the user. This takes place through the screen display and buttons on the unit.

User Segment
One segment of the entire GPS system that includes the GPS receiver.

Velocity Made Good (VMG)
The rate of closure to a destination, based upon your current speed and course.

Waypoint
A permanently stored and named position in the GPS receiver's memory.

Wide Area Augmentation System (WAAS)
A U.S. Federal Aviation Authority (FAA) system of equipment and software that supplements GPS accuracy, availability and integrity. The WAAS provides a satellite signal for WAAS users to support enroute and precision approach aircraft navigation.

WGS-84
World Geodetic System - 1984. The mathematical reference ellipsoid used by GPS.

Y-Code
The encrypted P-Code.

Electronics Aboard -- By Stephen Fishman

Electronics Aboard -- By Stephen Fishman

Appendix B
Satellite Telephone Glossary

Authentication
    The process of validating and identifying a caller as being a legitimate Globalstar user.

Automatic mode selection
    Based on this user-changeable setting, the phone automatically determines whether it should make a call in Globalstar or cellular modes, depending on availability.

Availability
    The probability of attaining a specified level of performance and maintaining that level for a scheduled period of time.

Band
    A related set of frequencies which use a contiguous portion of the spectrum, often for a similar application.

Bandwidth
    The range of frequencies, measured in hertz (Hz), that can pass over a given transmission channel. The bandwidth determines the rate at which information can be transmitted through the circuit.

Beam
    A portion of the satellite footprint at L-band and S-band. The satellite footprint is divided into 16 beams.

Electronics Aboard -- By Stephen Fishman

Bent-pipe
A signal relay scheme in which a terrestrial-based signal is sent to a satellite, which then relays the signal back to earth with minimal processing by the satellite.

Broadcast
A signal transmitted to all user terminals in a service area, or the process.

Call barring
This service can be used in several ways: for the barring of all incoming calls or incoming calls when roaming; similarly, all outgoing calls may be barred, all outgoing international calls, or all outgoing international except those directed back to the user's home country.

Call forwarding
Enables the caller to have incoming calls forwarded to a different telephone number (i.e. voicemail) under pre-determined conditions such as if the handset is busy, if calls are not answered within a certain period of time, or if the handset is unable to receive transmission for whatever reason. An unconditional call forwarding option is also available.

Call hold
This service allows the user to put a caller on hold to either answer another call or dial a second number. The user can alternate between, or terminate, either of the two calls.

Call transfer
Enables the subscriber to transfer a call to a third party. The call to be transferred may be an incoming or outgoing call.

Calling line ID
This service allows the subscriber to preview the incoming caller's phone number, if provided by the network, and if allowed by the caller.

Call waiting
Call waiting alerts the user of an incoming call when the user is already on the line. To receive the incoming

Electronics Aboard -- By Stephen Fishman

call, the first call can either be terminated or put on hold.

C-band

A band of frequencies in the 4 to 8 GHz frequency transmission range that are used for satellite and terrestrial communications.

CDMA (Code Division Multiple Access) A digital technology pioneered by QUALCOMM that provides crystal clear voice quality in an exciting new generation of wireless communications products and services. Using digital encoding and "spread spectrum" radio frequency (RF) techniques, CDMA provides much better cost-effective voice quality, privacy, system capacity, and flexibility than other wireless technologies, along with enhanced services such as short messaging, e-mail and Internet access.

CDMA (forward) circuit

A 1.23 MHz wide spread-spectrum signal (with a unique Walsh code) that resides within an FDM channel. It typically provides connection between the handset and the Gateway via the satellite.

Channel

A 1.23 MHz wide frequency band that contains multiple CDMA circuits.

Closed user group

This service enables users to be part of a group in which the members (i.e. employees of the same company) can place calls to each other but not to members outside of the group. Users may be a member of multiple groups. It is applicable to all services except emergency calling.

Connected line ID

This feature allows the calling party to have the called party's telephone number displayed on the handset. This service may also be restricted.

Coverage area

A geographical area, which moves in time with the

satellite, which defines the antenna coverage of a particular satellite.

Digital
Referring to communications techniques and procedures whereby information is encoded as binary language, as opposed analog representation of information in variable, but continuous, wave forms.

Downlink
The portion of a satellite circuit extending from the satellite to the user terminal. The Globalstar system establishes the service downlink in the S-band region of the frequency spectrum.

Dual mode
A handset which has the ability to operate on several frequencies and several types of communications systems. For example, the Globalstar system will have the capability of operating in either a cellular or satellite mode.

Feeder link sub-band
A frequency band 16.5 MHz wide that contains up to 13 FDM channels which corresponds to a single user-link antenna beam, and is a part of the feeder link band which is transmitted either to or from the satellite by a gateway antenna.

Feeder link band
A band of frequencies approximately 160 MHz wide containing contiguous feeder link sub-bands. There are 16 sub-bands on the uplink band and 16 on the downlink band. They are communicated as eight contiguous sub-bands on RHCP and eight on LHCP polarization, to or from the Gateway.

FDMA
Frequency Division Multiple Access (FDMA)- communicating devices at different locations sharing a multi-point or broadcast channel by means of a technique that allocates different frequencies to different users.

Electronics Aboard -- By Stephen Fishman

FDM channel
    A 1.23 MHz wide channel with a specific center frequency.

Finger
    An individual digital channel of a rake receiver. Also called "tine."

Footprint
    The portion of the earth's surface covered by the signal from a communications satellite.

Gateway link
    The link between the Gateway and the satellite.

Gaussian channel
    A channel whose only interference is white noise (AWGN-additive white gaussian noise).

Geo-synchronous orbit
    The orbit directly above the equator, about 35,800 kilometers (22,300 miles) above the earth in space. Also known as GEO, geo-stationary and Clarke orbit. When positioned in this orbit, a satellite appears to hover over the same spot on the earth because it is moving at a rate that matches the speed of the earth's rotation on its axis.

Hand off
    The process of transferring a subscriber call from one satellite to another.

Inclination angle
    The angle at which a satellite orbit is tilted relative to the earth's equator. For example, Globalstar satellites are at a 52-degree inclination.

Ka-Band
    A band of frequencies in the 18 to 31 GHz range that are available for global satellite use.

Ku-Band
    A band of frequencies in the 10.9 to 17 GHz range that are used for fixed satellite service applications.

L-band
    A band of frequencies in the 0.5 to 2 GHz range that

Electronics Aboard -- By Stephen Fishman

are used primarily for voice communications.

Low earth orbit
A satellite that orbits 400 to 1,600 miles (644 to 2,575 kilometers) above the earth's surface. 48 to 66 LEOs are needed to cover the entire earth.

Medium earth orbit (MEO)
An earth orbit in an altitude roughly midway between the earth and geo-synchronous orbit. Satellite orbits between the altitudes of 1,500 and 6,500 kilometers (930 to 4040 miles) may be considered MEOs.

Network
A term used to describe various communication interconnections. There is a communication network, a SOCC network, a GOCC network, and the public switched telephone network. There are also others in the system.

Orbital slot
A slot above the equator that corresponds to a particular longitude position and can be occupied by five to ten geo-stationary satellites.

Path diversity
An exclusive feature of the Globalstar system that allows several satellites to pick up an individual call. This assures that the call does not get dropped even if a phone moves out of sight of one of the satellites.

PLMN
Public Land Mobile Network

PSTN
Public Switched Telephone Network

PTT
Postal, Telegraph and Telephone organization (PTT) -- usually a governmental department that acts as its nation's common carrier.

Phasing orbit
Temporary orbit used prior to injection of satellite into final orbit.

Rake receiver
Receiver having a number of individual digital channels (tines) which can combine these channels to form a stronger received signal.

Registration
The process of locating a UT to determine which Gateway should serve it.

Return traffic circuit
A CDMA circuit to a Gateway from a user carrying user traffic and other in-band signaling. Each of these is distinguished by a unique time offset of the long code.

Roaming
The ability of a subscriber to travel worldwide, and subject to certain limitations, make and receive telephone calls -- particularly outside the service area of the subscriber's telecommunications service provider.

Satellite
An active electronic communications device placed into orbit around the earth consisting of a payload and bus or platform.

S-band
The portion of the electromagnetic spectrum allotted for transmission in the 2 to 4 GHz frequency range.

Service area
A geographical area on the ground that is the minimum covered by a gateway and its associated satellites. It is normally operated by a service provider.

Service link
The links between the UT and the satellite.

Service provider
An entity that operates and/or owns one or more gateways and provides services to customers of telecommunications system.

Short message service (SMS)
SMS allows users to transmit short text messages of up to 160 characters. If the user if unreachable, the message will be stored in the message center until it can

Electronics Aboard -- By Stephen Fishman

be accessed.

Short-term fade
A fade whose duration is less than the round-trip delay (including path delay) from the Gateway to the user.

Soft handoff
The process of transferring a circuit from one beam or satellite to another without interruption of the call.

Telemetry, tracking and control (TT&C)
These three functions control and monitor a group of satellites.

Transponder
Component of a communications satellite that receives a signal from earth, processes and amplifies it, and then re-transmits it to another location on earth.

Uplink
The portion of a satellite circuit extending from the user terminal to the satellite. The Globalstar system establishes the service uplink in the L-Band.

User terminal (UT)
Used by subscribers to communicate via satellite telecommunications system. User terminals include hand-held user terminals powered from internal batteries, mobile units powered from a vehicle battery, or fixed station units powered from fixed prime power sources.

Wireline
Terrestrially-based telephone line.

Electronics Aboard -- *By Stephen Fishman*

Appendix C
Table of Figures

Figure 1-1: Edson multiple antenna mount
Figure 1-2: Surface-mount electronics
Figure 1-3: Modern flybridge instrumentation
Figure 1-4: Electronics for a short cruise
Figure 1-5: Electronics for an extended cruise
Figure 1-6: Instruments mounted on a pedestal guard
Figure 1-7: Enclosed sailboat helm
Figure 1-8: Instrument installations forward of the cockpit
Figure 1-9: Surface-mount wiring seal
Figure 2-1: Raymarine's Autohelm system
Figure 2-2: SeaTalk wiring
Figure 2-3: Furuno NavNet
Figure 2-4: Ethernet BNC connector
Figure 2-5: DB-25 male connector
Figure 3-1: Monochrome green CRT display
Figure 3-2: LED multiple display
Figure 3-3: Modern LCD color display
Figure 3-4: Raymarine ST40 speed and depth display
Figure 3-5: Icom Model 710 single sideband radio
Figure 3-6: Simrad CA-40 radar/chartplotter
Figure 3-7: PinPoint Systems LCD marine displays
Figure 3-8: Flat screen LCD on a flybridge
Figure 4-1: VHF radio broadcast
Figure 4-2: Fixed-mount VHF radio
Figure 4-3: Hand-held VHF radio
Figure 4-4: Flush-mount

Electronics Aboard -- By Stephen Fishman

Figure 4-5: Wavelength range
Figure 5-1: Transom transducer
Figure 5-2: Wet but not too deep
Figure 5-3: Through-hull transducer
Figure 5-4: Various transducer locations
Figure 5-5: Commercial grade fishfinder
Figure 5-6: Color CRT display
Figure 5-7: LCD flat color display
Figure 6-1: Typical small scale electronic chart (Maptech)
Figure 6-2: Sample tide table display (The Cap'n)
Figure 6-3: Graphical tides display (Maptech)
Figure 6-4: Toolbar comparison
Figure 7-1: Typical chartplotter
Figure 7-2: Chartplotter display
Figure 7-3: Integrated DGPS chartplotter
Figure 7-4: Raytheon model 425 chartplotter controls
Figure 7-5: Typical screen display and chart outlines
Figure 8-1: Electronic compass locations
Figure 8-2: Wheel pilot
Figure 8-3: Below-deck pilot
Figure 8-4: Autopilot control module
Figure 9-1: Harbor buoy
Figure 9-2: Open array antenna
Figure 9-3: Radome antenna
Figure 9-4: CRT display
Figure 9-5: LCD color display
Figure 10-1: U.S. South Central Loran coverage
Figure 10-2: New Foundland and British Columbia Loran
Figure 10-3: Three common chain configurations
Figure 10-4: A Loran position fix
Figure 10-5: Furuno LC90 MK2 Loran-C receiver
Figure 11-1: GPS satellite
Figure 11-2: GPS network
Figure 11-3: Relative orbits of satellites
Figure 11-4: Single broadcasting satellite
Figure 11-5: Poor satellite geometry
Figure 11-6: Good satellite geometry

Electronics Aboard -- *By Stephen Fishman*

Figure 11-7: WAAS coverage map
Figure 11-8: WAAS system
Figure 12-1: Skywave reflections
Figure 12-2: Typical SSB
Figure 12-3: Sideband remote unit
Figure 12-4: Creating a groundplane
Figure 12-5: Copper screen and radials
Figure 13-1: Furuno weatherfax
Figure 13-2: Common symbols of a weather chart
Figure 13-3: Common weather map symbols
Figure 13-4: Wind speed and direction indicators
Figure 14-1: Satellite telephone
Figure 14-2: Globalstar coverage map
Figure 14-3: Globalstar cellular/satellite phone
Figure 15-1: Wire size chart
Figure 15-2: Loop drip wiring
Figure 15-3: Solder splices
Figure 15-4: Mechanical butt splice
Figure 15-5: Ring and spade terminals
Figure 15-6: Common hand tools for electrical projects

Electronics Aboard -- By Stephen Fishman

Books published by
Bristol Fashion Publications
Free catalog, phone 1-800-478-7147

Boat Repair Made Easy — Haul Out
Written By John P. Kaufman

Boat Repair Made Easy — Finishes
Written By John P. Kaufman

Boat Repair Made Easy — Systems
Written By John P. Kaufman

Boat Repair Made Easy — Engines
Written By John P. Kaufman

Standard Ship's Log
Designed By John P. Kaufman

Large Ship's Log
Designed By John P. Kaufman

Designing Power & Sail
Written By Arthur Edmunds

Building A Fiberglass Boat
Written By Arthur Edmunds

Buying A Great Boat
Written By Arthur Edmunds

Boater's Book of Nautical Terms
Written By David S. Yetman

Electronics Aboard -- By Stephen Fishman

Practical Seamanship
Written By David S. Yetman

Creating Comfort Afloat
Written By Janet Groene

Living Aboard
Written By Janet Groene

Racing The Ice To Cape Horn
Written By Frank Guernsey & Cy Zoerner

Marine Weather Forecasting
Written By J. Frank Brumbaugh

Complete Guide To Gasoline Marine Engines
Written By John Fleming

Complete Guide To Outboard Engines
Written By John Fleming

Complete Guide To Diesel Marine Engines
Written By John Fleming

Trouble Shooting Gasoline Marine Engines
Written By John Fleming

Trailer Boats
Written By Alex Zidock

Skipper's Handbook
Written By Robert S. Grossman

White Squall - The Last Voyage Of Albatross
Written By Richard E. Langford

Electronics Aboard -- By Stephen Fishman

Cruising South
What to Expect Along the ICW
Written By Joan Healy

Electronics Aboard
Written By Stephen Fishman

Five Against The Sea
A True Story of Courage & Survival
Written By Ron Arias

Scuttlebutt
Seafaring History & Lore
Written By John Guest

Cruising The South Pacific
Written By Douglas Austin

Catch of The Day
How To Catch, Clean & Cook Seafood
Written By Carla Johnson

Electronics Aboard -- By Stephen Fishman

About The Author

Stephen Fishman has been sailing for the better part of the last quarter century. Through this experience, he has become a well-known writer and speaker. Stephen was a successful yacht broker and, for many years, owned a full-service yacht repair and maintenance company that serviced pleasure boats in Clear Lake, Texas.

In 1994, Stephen began writing and illustrating a monthly repair column for *Telltales Magazine*, a Texas coastal sailing publication. Within a few years, he established monthly columns in *Gulf Coast Moorings, Southwinds* and *Dockside Magazine*. Along with his monthly columns, his articles have also been published in *Yachting Magazine, Southern Boating, Chesapeake Bay Magazine, Motorboating* and many others.

Stephen has also accepted larger assignments, such as the user manual for *The Cap'n*, a software navigation program used by pleasure boaters as well as the U.S. military.

In 1999 many of his projects were collected in a book titled **Boat Improvements for the Practical Sailor**, published by Sheridan House.

He is a certified instructor for the Texas Parks and Wildlife Boater's Safety Course, a scuba diving teaching assistant and certified Divemaster. He splits his spare time between sailing on Galveston Bay, riding his motorcycle and playing percussion with a variety of local bands.

Stephen and his wife, Deborah, lived aboard *Lady Greyhawke*, their Catalina 320, on the upper Galveston Bay for six years.

www.ingramcontent.com/pod-product-compliance
Lightning Source LLC
Chambersburg PA
CBHW032021230426
43671CB00005B/155